Translated from the Russian and edited by

MICHAEL GLENNY

With an Introduction by

ISAAC DEUTSCHER

HILL AND WANG · New York

REVOLUTIONARY SILHOUETTES

Anatoly Vasilievich Lunacharsky

This translation first published in 1967
by Allen Lane The Penguin Press

Published in the United States of America by Hill and Wang, Inc.
Library of Congress catalog card number: 68-30764

First American Edition September 1968

Printed in the United States of America

1234567890

CONTENTS

Photo credits:

Lunacharsky, Sverdlov, Volodarsky: Novosti Press Agency

Lenin, Trotsky, Zinoviev, Uritsky, Martov:

Radio Times Hulton Picture Library

Plekhanov: Paul Popper

*The Editor records with gratitude
the assistance given by Dr Harold Shukman
of St Antony's College, Oxford.*

LIST OF ILLUSTRATIONS

INTRODUCTION

by Isaac Deutscher

The name of Anatoly Vasilievich Lunacharsky is not well remembered in the West and is probably not very widely known at present even in Russia. Yet he was one of the most famous leaders of the Revolution, and its first great Commissar of Education. His influence, even if submerged, has survived in Soviet cultural life; and a new generation of the Soviet intelligentsia is discovering in him one of its spiritual ancestors.

Born in Poltava in 1875, he grew up in the environment of the minor nobility, under the influence of well-educated, radically minded, people. His father was a notary. 'I became,' he says, 'a revolutionary so early in my life that I don't even remember when I was not one. My childhood passed under the strong influence of Alexander Ivanovich Antonov [his mother's friend] who, though "an acting privy counsellor" and head of the Control Chamber of Nizhni Novgorod, and then of Kursk . . . did not at all conceal his leanings towards radical and left aspirations.' The environment was similar to that in which Lenin grew up, though it was less provincial than Lenin's and more advanced politically. Lunacharsky grew up in Kiev. The city was a meeting point of Russian, Polish, Jewish and Ukrainian cultures, and an important centre of radical and socialist movements. The school boy, a voracious reader, precocious and gifted, was very early drawn into a clandestine Marxist circle; he helped to expand it until 200 pupils adhered to it. Earlier than elsewhere in the Tsar's Empire the Marxists there prevailed against the Populists, and Marxism became the adolescent's intellectual love affair; it was to last all his life. But he was equally attracted, very early, by another intellectual current; namely, the philosophy of empirio-criticism, especially the theories of the German-Swiss Professor, Avenarius. In 1894, Lunacharsky left Russia for

Switzerland, and sat at Avenarius's feet at Zürich University. That year left ineradicable marks on his outlook. Henceforth his ambition was to reconcile the influences of Marx and Avenarius. He was convinced that Marxism needed to be 'propped up' philosophically and that empirio-criticism was best suited to do that. In Zürich he met Axelrod and Plekhanov, the founders and leading lights of Russian Marxism. They frowned upon his philosophical 'foible'. He listened and learned from them, especially from Plekhanov, but stuck to his Avenarius. In Western European colonies of Russian exiles and students he soon became known as an outstanding lecturer and gifted orator, astonishingly erudite for his age. (At the university he took courses in anatomy, zoology, psychology, philosophy and political economy.) Among his fellow-students was Rosa Luxemburg, presently to become famous in European socialism as the most brilliant opponent of the revisionists and reformists during the great debate in the German Social Democratic Party. Even at the university, Lunacharsky recalls, 'I respected her greatly and was, in a way, captivated by her. I was charmed by something fairy-like and slightly devilish in her tiny, almost dwarf-like, figure with the big expressive head on her feeble shoulders.' Among the old *émigrés*, Lavrov the inspirer of Russian populism and Marx's friend was approaching the end of his life: he 'lived in something like a cave dug out among books; he . . . seemed to me a prodigy of encyclopaedic knowledge. I still managed to have with him long and interesting discussions on matters that interested me then more than anything else, the origins of tribal myths among various peoples remote from one another, and the rules governing the evolution of those myths.' None of these diverse interests weakened the young man's revolutionary zeal. On the contrary, to be active as a revolutionary he needed to view society from every possible angle. Such was his fervour that he converted his gravely ill and paralysed brother to his views and drew him into revolutionary activity first in France and then in Russia. Very soon, however, his empirio-critical ideas brought him into conflict with Plekhanov, whose 'orthodoxy' was to Lunacharsky's mind 'dry and too rationalistic'. Plekhanov's attempts to link Marxism philosophically to the tradition of the French Enlightenment, especially to Diderot and d'Holbach was to him 'flat and unsatisfactory'.

In 1896 Lunacharsky returned (with his brother) to Russia. He went to Moscow and there at once joined a clandestine group, which, after many arrests carried out by the police, was trying to build up a new social-democratic organization. One member of the group was Anna Elizarova, Lenin's elder sister. (Lenin himself, still little known, was at the threshold of his revolutionary career.) Soon, however, Lunacharsky was arrested – it turned out that the police had an *agent-provocateur* in the group. He was held in solitary confinement for eight months and then deported to the north to Kaluga, Vologda, and other places.

For his further fortunes his stay at Kaluga was particularly important, for there he met A. A. Bogdanov [Malinovsky] who was to become his closest friend and political and philosophical associate (and whose sister he married). Bogdanov, now unjustly forgotten, was one of the most original and impressive figures in the Russian revolutionary movement. For a few crucial years, between 1903 and 1908, Lenin's close political companion, and, at times, his second-in-command, Bogdanov was a man of rare nobility, heroic strength of character, and many-sided intellectual gifts. He made his mark as an economist and author of a famous textbook; he was the outstanding Russian exponent of the empirio-critical or empiriomonist philosophy; as a political leader he inspired a special trend in Bolshevism; and as an art critic he was to become the originator of the idea of proletarian culture [Proletkult]. He was also an outstanding doctor and pioneering research worker – he was to die, in 1928, while carrying out a dangerous medical experiment on himself. Bogdanov confirmed Lunacharsky in his striving for a synthesis between Marxism and Avenarius's philosophy.

In the places of their deportation in the North, the

exiles, benefiting from the aid and sympathy of local society, studied, lectured and contributed to various periodicals. Lunacharsky engaged in public debate against, among others, Berdiayev, a co-exile, who at this time was already moving away from Marxism and embracing Christianity. The theme of their controversy was religion and socialism; and although Lunacharsky, to the Marxists' satisfaction, zestfully assailed Berdiayev's views, he was himself somewhat 'touched' by his opponent's ideas. The police, alarmed by these debates, deported Lunacharsky farther north towards Archangel, where he was almost completely isolated. He used his enforced solitude to write one of his most original works, *The Experience of Positive Aesthetics*. He translated many European, especially German, poets, and published a great deal of literary criticism. In his treatise on aesthetics, he not only tried to combine empirio-criticism with dialectical materialism, but he strongly emphasized the biological and physiological basis of aesthetic sensitivity. He was criticized on the grounds that he neglected the social conditioning of art, but he was, in fact, arguing well within the Marxist way of thinking. In later years he demonstrated effectively the special validity of his views in analysing the physiological and biological factors in the development of music.

Having served his term, Lunacharsky returned, in 1901 or 1902, to Kiev where one of the radical liberal periodicals offered him the post of dramatic critic. But he could not keep that post for long. In 1903 all socialist circles were agog with the split that had just occurred in Western Europe between Mensheviks and Bolsheviks. The shock was so great that in Russia many Bolsheviks had second thoughts and sought a reunion. Lenin, however, held out; and among the few who supported him unreservedly was Bogdanov. The latter urged Lunacharsky to come to Switzerland and help in editing a militant Bolshevik periodical. Lunacharsky responded to the call, although he had his doubts and mental reservations. His first contacts with Lenin, which occurred in Paris and Geneva in 1904, did not leave him with the most pleasant of memories. To the theorist of 'positive aesthetics', Lenin was too exclusively absorbed in politics and too much down to earth. Lunacharsky, nevertheless, became a militant Bolshevik: not so much from the conviction that Lenin was right as from the feeling that the Mensheviks were wrong – that they obstructed the revolutionary movement from the inside, and dragged it down to sheer opportunism and compromise.

He himself described his early association with Lenin in the following frank reminiscence, which appeared after the revolution: 'of course there was a great discord [of character] between myself and Lenin. He approached all issues as a man of political action with an immense audacity of spirit, as a tactician and indeed as a political leader of genius, whereas my approach was that of the philosopher, or, to put it more accurately, the poet of the revolution. To me the revolution was a stage, inevitably tragic, in the world-wide development of the human spirit toward the "Universal Soul", the greatest and most decisive act in the process of "God-building", the most striking and definite deed in the realization of the programme which Nietzsche had so felicitously formulated when he said, "there is no sense in the world, but we ought to give sense to it".'

Reading these words one has no difficulty in imagining Lunacharsky, if he had lived forty or fifty years later, as some kind of a leftish existentialist, arguing about the 'absurdity of man's condition' and seeking to 'humanize' Marxism. No doubt, he was extremely sensitive to the philosophical and aesthetic fashions of the day; and to intellectuals of his generation Nietzsche and Avenarius were what, say, Heidegger and Sartre have been to some of our contemporaries. But as at that time it was not easy to impugn the humane character of revolutionary Marxism, some of its adherents sought not to 'humanize' but to 'deify' it. Lunacharsky was at pains to point out that his 'God-seeking' implied no belief in any supernatural power or idea. 'I preached,' he said, 'a tragic and active religion without any trace of "faith" or "mysticism".' Plekhanov, the Menshevik and the purist of Marxist philosophy thundered at this heresy. Lenin respected and accepted Plekhanov's judgement in these matters. Asked once what he thought of someone declaring that 'socialism is my religion', he replied, with much dialectical wit, that it all depended who made the statement; 'If a religious person made it he was saying in effect that he was abandoning religion for socialism. But if someone who considered himself a Marxist claimed socialism as his religion he was abandoning socialism for religion.' It did not, however, occur to Lenin to start a *political* quarrel over a philosophical issue; and Lunacharsky, at any rate, showed no sign of abandoning socialism (or even Bolshevism) for the sake of religion. And so he became a member of that small Bolshevik editorial team which brought out two papers *Forward* and *The Proletarian* – apart from Lenin and Lunacharsky there were only two other members on the staff. Lunacharsky, writing under the pen name Voinov (Fighter), demonstrated his militancy not only in debates and skirmishes with the Mensheviks, but also at party congress, an exclusively Bolshevik one, at which he was *rapporteur* on armed insurrection and its place in socialist strategy. His heart, however, was still in poetry and the arts rather than in strategy and tactics. It remained there even during the revolution of 1905, in which he played no outstanding role. Like Lenin himself, he returned to Russia too late when the revolution was already ebbing away. During his brief spell in St Petersburg, he co-edited, with Maxim Gorky, *Novaya Zhizn* [New Life] a Bolshevik daily, the first to be published in the open. His lectures, mostly on literary and artistic themes, drew such immense crowds that the entrance fees made quite a substantial contribution to Lenin's not-too-rich party chest.

Lunacharsky's breach with Lenin came later, in 1908, in the period of defeat and reaction. They were once again *émigrés* in Western Europe and their disheartened followers in Russia had very nearly dispersed. Lenin urged his party to hold out, to dig in deep in the underground, but to work also in the open, lawfully, wherever the opportunity offered itself. 'We must now learn the arts of retreat,' he often said, realistic and determined as ever. He argued, on the one hand, against those among the Mensheviks who wanted to have an open party with no underground activities at all; and, on the other, against the 'ultra-lefts', the romantic revolutionaries, among his own comrades, notably Lunacharsky and Bogdanov, who were reluctant to learn the 'arts of retreat'. Bogdanov and Lunacharsky pressed Lenin to disavow the socialist members of the Duma (the Tsar's quasi-parliament) who, in their view, behaved all too timidly and adjusted themselves to triumphant reaction. Lenin refused to come out in this way against the socialist parliamentarians; and consequently the ultra-leftists attacked him as an 'opportunist' and 'semi-Menshevik'.

The quarrel over tactics was soon followed by the great philosophical controversy in the course of which Lenin wrote his *Materialism and Empirio-Criticism.* Lunacharsky's major contribution to this controversy consisted in his two volumes of *Socialism and Religion* which again met with Plekhanov's severe rebuff.

Lenin had long avoided this controversy, and now he embarked on it reluctantly. He did so because the Mensheviks made the most of the fact that the philosophical 'deviators' from Marxism, the 'God-seekers' and Empiriocritics were mostly Bolsheviks. Setting themselves up as guardians of Marxist orthodoxy, the Mensheviks used this circumstance to discredit Lenin and his followers. Lenin countered by dissociating himself from Lunacharsky's and Bogdanov's philosophical as well as political views, and by subjecting these to stringent criticism. He had been prepared to tolerate almost any philosophical or religious 'heresy' within the party in the interest of political unity. But now that the political unity had broken down anyhow, and the Bogdanov–Lunacharsky group had come out against him in the open, he had no reason to remain reticent about the philosophical disagreements. He was also convinced that Bogdanov's and Lunacharsky's ultra leftism were not unconnected with their philosophical 'deviation'. However, neither Plekhanov's nor Lenin's arguments against empirio-criticism made much impression on Lunacharsky who stuck to his views to the end.

Of the tedious three- or four-cornered interfactional struggles that went on until the First World War one incident may be recalled here. Lunacharsky and Bogdanov found an ally in Maxim Gorky who was then at the height of his fame as a novelist and playwright. The three of them established at Capri, in Italy, a 'party school', to which they brought workers from Russia, whom they instructed in economic theory, history, and the arts, and whom they initiated into 'God-seeking' and, no doubt, turned against Lenin's rightist 'semi-Menshevik' policy. Lenin denied them the right to describe these courses as a 'party school'. He denounced the venture as a factional intrigue, and he managed to disrupt it by converting some of Lunacharsky's pupils. Lunacharsky then opened a new school at Bologna, which, with such teachers as himself, Gorky, Trotsky, Pokrovsky, the historian, and others, attracted new worker pupils. (Lunacharsky himself conducted the workers on tours through the museums and art galleries of Italy hoping to inject something of the spirit of Renaissance art into the cadres of the Russian revolution.) Lenin set up his own school at Longjumeau, near Paris, where with fewer eminent teachers, and a more down-to-earth curriculum, he trained future leaders and commissars far more successfully. Despite the disputes and quarrels, however, he remained on friendly terms with Lunacharsky and, of course, Gorky. With Lenin's agreement, Lunacharsky acted as the Bolsheviks' spokesman at various international socialist congresses. And despite Lenin's severe censuring of Bogdanov's views, he treated Lunacharsky's 'deviation' with an amiable irony. The story was told how at one meeting after Lunacharsky had preached 'God-seeking', Lenin approached him with lowered head and, with a malicious glint in his eye, whispered: 'Bless me, Father Anatol.'

The outbreak of the First World War overshadowed all these disputes and *émigrés*' squabbles. Lunacharsky was then in Paris and, with Trotsky and Martov, coedited a Russian daily which voiced opposition to the war and supported the so-called Zimmerwald movement – the forerunner of the Communist International. In 1915, after the French government closed the paper and expelled Trotsky from France, Lunacharsky moved over to Switzerland where Lenin was campaigning against the war. He did not as yet rejoin the Bolsheviks. In 1917, when shortly after the February revolution he returned to Russia, he joined the so-called *Mezhrayontsy* in Petrograd – a group which was led by Trotsky – and it was with Trotsky and that group that he re-entered the Bolshevik party in August of that year.

His role in the events of 1917 was quite outstanding, as all eye-witnesses testify. The 'soft' 'God-seeker' with the air of the absent-minded professor, surprised and astonished all who saw him by his indomitable militancy and energy. He was the great orator of Red Petrograd, second only to Trotsky, addressing every day, or even several times a day, huge, hungry and angry crowds of workers, soldiers and sailors, and breaking down almost effortlessly, by his sheer sincerity and sensitivity, all barriers of social origin and education that might have separated him from them. The crowds were spellbound by him and loved him. In July when Kerensky's government ordered the imprisonment of most Bolshevik leaders, under charges of conspiracy and espionage for Germany, Lunacharsky too was imprisoned. After two months, however, he was at large, speaking again for his party in the Soviet, in the factories and in the barracks, and rallying mass support for the coming insurrection. So large did he loom in those fateful days that later, after the revolution, people were puzzled to see him playing a relatively smaller role. What in truth prevented Lunacharsky, for all his energy, his vast erudition and high intelligence, from holding the position of one of the very first leaders of Bolshevism was probably a certain excess of generosity and a certain lack of inwardly concentrated thought and will power. It is not for nothing that in his character profiles of the Bolshevik leaders, Lenin, Trotsky, Sverdlov, and others, the quality of these people which he emphasizes and admires most is their powerful and concentrated will, the quality in which he was deficient – he was indeed the very opposite of the so-called single-track mind. In 1917 when the revolution worked like a phenomenon of nature with all its elements unleashed, he merged with it and rose to its height.

Lenin when he made the appointments for his first government chose Lunacharsky, without a moment's hesitation, for the post of the Commissar of Education. He showed himself in this the great judge of men he was, and the choice of the person was also a choice of policy. 'In matters of culture,' Lenin used to say, 'nothing is as harmful and pernicious as hate, arrogance and fanaticism. In these matters great care and tolerance must be exercised.' He preferred as the Commissar of Education the 'soft' deviationist and God-seeker rather than any of his more orthodox and tougher comrades, although he knew well that Lunacharsky was no administrator at all. Like a good conductor discerning the strength and weakness of each player in his orchestra, Lenin almost unfailingly distributed the instruments. There was, of course, no question of Lunacharsky having to retract any of his philosophical heresies, or to apologize for any of his political vagaries – such rituals were simply unthinkable in the Lenin era; they were to be introduced later.

Although Lunacharsky was not, after 1917, among the party's top leaders, his role in the constructive work of the new regime was first rate. The revolution had to take over the 'cultural heritage' of the past, to preserve it, to make it accessible to the masses as it had never been before, to educate them and develop them culturally; to bring the socialist spirit into the work of education; and to experiment and innovate. Lunacharsky combined in himself almost ideally the qualities of the guardian of the heritage and those of the innovator. It was characteristic of him that after a few days in office he resigned in order to protest against the alleged firing by the Red Guards at the Kremlin in Moscow, during the October insurrection, which had damaged its walls. He published a fiery Manifesto denouncing this 'act of vandalism', and appealed to the working class to take under its protection all architectural monuments and treasures of art. He resumed office only after he was reassured that the Kremlin had suffered no damage during the insurrection.

His first and most elementary task was to insure that the schools and cultural institutions should function without interruption. This was not easy, because many teachers, intellectuals and professional people refused to work under the 'Bolshevik usurpers'. Lunacharsky was indefatigable in talking them out of the boycott; he largely succeeded. His devotion to education and to the sciences and arts was known; his bearing and manner inspired confidence. He was often described as the 'intellectual among the Bolsheviks, and the Bolshevik among the intellectuals'. Although the description may not be quite accurate, for most of the Bolshevik leaders were 'intellectuals', Lunacharsky was nevertheless exceptionally convincing in his dealings with the anti-Bolshevik and 'neutral' intelligentsia. Lenin, who saw clearly that, without the intelligentsia's willing support, the revolution could hardly safeguard its cultural heritage, assisted Lunacharsky in every way. Academicians and scientists were accorded as ample facilities for work as could be secured in the years of foreign intervention, civil war, hunger and privation. Lunacharsky was also superb in his struggle against illiteracy, and in 'carrying to the masses' music, drama, literature and the visual arts. He did not flatter the tastes of workers and peasants, but sought to educate them aesthetically. He modernized the basic educational system, opening the doors of the school wide to the fresh breath of the revolution. He reformed the teaching methods in a progressive libertarian spirit, putting into effect Marxist conceptions and frankly borrowing ideas from advanced foreign 'bourgeois' thinkers. (A glimpse of the Soviet schools was enough to arouse enthusiasm in so critical an educationist as John Dewey, the eminent American philosopher.)

In his endeavours to carry the cultural heritage to the masses and to educate them aesthetically, he sometimes had to make a noble sacrifice and descend from his heights of intellectual sophistication in order to speak plainly and simply about complex historical or literary trends. He does this, for instance, in his *Highlights of Western European Literature*, a series of lectures he gave in the early twenties at the Sverdlov University to workers and soldiers whom the party had drawn from the ranks to promote them to economic, administrative and military posts.

He did not, however, promote popularization at the expense of originality and experimentation. Under his auspices, the 'hundred flowers' really blossomed; many artistic schools, coteries, and isms, some quite hermetic and esoteric, flourished. Yet as a critic he himself was an outspoken partisan. But as the Commissar, dispensing state patronage, he was a fair and judicious umpire. It wouldn't have occurred to him to impose his views or tastes on anybody. He himself wrote volumes of literary criticism on Pushkin, Gogol, Tolstoy, Dostoyevsky, Andreyev, Gorky and others; and he fostered a national cult of the classics. At the same time, he backed, to Lenin's and Trotsky's mortification, the Proletcult, whose adherents advocated a breach with all classical tradition, and the advent of the proletarian epoch in art and literature. Very early he sponsored Picasso's works in Russia (the works which have ever since his days been stored away in the cellars of the Soviet museums). He encouraged Tatlin, the great architect, who might be described as Russia's Corbusier, were it not for his far more extreme 'modernism'. He appointed Chagall director of the popular Academy of Art at Vitebsk, and allowed the same scope to Malevsky, the constructivist and Chagall's bitter opponent. He acted the godfather to Meyerhold's 'bio-mechanical' theatre and to Eisenstein's epoch-making film projects. The Futurists, the Serapion Brothers, the Constructivists, the Imaginists – all benefited from his generosity, even while Lenin frowned at the large printings of Mayakovsky's poems at the time of an acute paper shortage. He helped to bring to life the famous *Habima*, the first Hebrew theatre in history, though many Jews, communists and non-communists alike, protested against the resuscitation – in Red Russia! – of Hebrew, then a dead language, and against the idealization of the religious – Hassidic – legend of the Dybbuk on its stage. Lunacharsky shrugged: nothing in mankind's artistic heritage was alien to him; and in this case the innovator in him was at one with the guardian of old values. What astronomical distance separates spiritually that period not only from the severe barbarity of the Stalin era, but even from the desiccated bureaucratic 'liberalism' of the post-Stalin years! No wonder that nowadays Soviet writers and artists, old and young, hark back to that first post-revolutionary decade as to something like a 'golden age', and draw from it inspiration. Though this was too brief and stormy a period for great 'monumental' art to mature, it nevertheless stirred profoundly Russia's sensitivity and poetic imagination. By the end of the decade, however, the icy lid of the monolith had begun to descend upon artistic creation as upon anything else.

Lunacharsky did not participate in the grim inner party struggle which followed Lenin's death. He felt lost amid its intricacies, intrigues and *mores*. To none of the contestants had he been as close as to Trotsky whom he describes, in the character sketch included in this volume, as belonging with Lenin to 'the two strongest of the strong, totally identified with their roles'. But he had misgivings about Trotsky's 'prickly and overbearing' character and lack of talent for team work; and knowing how strong the feeling against Trotsky ran in the old Bolshevik guard, he probably guessed that Trotsky was fighting a losing battle. He tried to adjust himself to Zinoviev, for whom he had far less respect and admiration than for Trotsky, but who had long been Lenin's close companion and whom, in 1923–5, many regarded as the 'strong helmsman'.

Of Lunacharsky's 'adjustment' to Stalin there could be no question. No two characters were or could be more alien to each other and more incompatible than these two. The lack of any human or political bond between them is evidenced by this series of Lunacharsky's character-sketches of the Bolshevik leaders. A huge gap yawned from it at Russian readers: the book contained no character sketch of Stalin. When it was published in 1923, and reprinted in 1924, the struggle for Lenin's succession was at its height; and Stalin was already well-established as the party's general secretary. The omission amounted to *lèse-majesté*. And so shortly thereafter the book 'vanished from circulation' – it remained banned for forty years. (Only in the last few years parts of it, carefully selected and censored, have been republished.) It is inconceivable that Lunacharsky should not have been aware how loudly his silence about Stalin spoke. Evidently, he could not bring himself to pay even the most perfunctory homage to the General Secretary. He was in effect telling his fellow-Bolsheviks that he was prepared to serve, if he must, under Zinoviev, but not under Stalin.

When Stalin finally came to the top, Lunacharsky decided to ignore him as far as possible, to keep aloof from inner-party affairs, and to shut himself up in his educational and literary work. He shunned the conventicles at which the warring factions stormed against one another and party meetings which were the spectacles of the degrading 'personality cult'. He still hoped to keep some autonomy in his own domain, to save education, literature and the arts from the bulldozers of Stalinism, and to go on with the job of a socialist *Kulturträger*. His prolific pen beat all its records in these years. He published his *Art and Revolution* and *Theatre and Revolution* as well as the *Highlights of Western European Literature* in 1924; *From Spinoza to Marx* in 1925; *Problems of the Sociology of Music* in 1927, various collections of critical essays, not to speak of film scripts and dramas.*

But even the Commissariat and his writer's study could not afford him the sanctuary he sought. The Commissariat was gradually infiltrated by Stalin's agents; and, in any case, the General Secretary did not at all favour Lunacharsky's 'semi-anarchist' educational experiments and the 'decadent modernistic' uproar in literature and the arts. Slowly the new discipline was being enforced. Then

* He had written a play, *Oliver Cromwell*, in 1919, *Campanelli* in 1922, and later, in the twenties, he published his dramatic works in two volumes. I have not read his plays, but I remember that critics in Moscow spoke of them with condescending irony and considered him a mediocre playwright.

in 1927 Trotsky, Rakovsky and Radek were exiled to Siberia while Zinoviev and Kamenev were to all intents and purposes expelled from the party. Lunacharsky was deeply unhappy. His anguished heart was failing him, and he practically ceased to attend to his official duties, although nominally he still remained at the head of the Commissariat for another two years, until 1929. He found some relief in temporary assignments abroad; he acted as the Soviet spokesman on cultural affairs at the League of Nations in Geneva, and used the occasions to roam, with his old friend, Maxim Litvinov, who presently became Commissar of Foreign Affairs, his old haunts in Europe, the museums and theatres of Paris and Berlin. He felt more and more a stranger in Moscow, amid the bizarre orgies of the Stalin cult and the violence of the 'wholesale' collectivization; after every return there he slipped away again to Western Europe to cure his incurable heart and to get a rest for his oppressed mind. From France and Germany he still sent literary-critical essays and correspondences, sadly impoverished in content and cramped in style, for Soviet periodicals. From everywhere the blows were falling: in 1931 the second of Russia's two outstanding poets of the revolutionary epoch, Mayakovsky, committed suicide – Esenin had done the same a few years earlier. In 1932 Stalin berated the party historians who were not zealous enough in falsifying the history of the revolution. And then, in 1933, Germany was plunged headlong into the abyss of Nazism. A glimmer of hope, however, had appeared at the other end of Europe, with the rise of the Republic in Spain. Lunacharsky was appointed Ambassador to Madrid. Was the appointment made on Litvinov's or on Stalin's initiative? In the light of later events the assignment may have been ominous, for in subsequent years the Madrid Embassy became something of a death chamber to its holders, who on their return to Moscow as a rule perished in the great purges. Lunacharsky died in his fifty-ninth year before he managed to take up his post. (He had spent his last weeks trying to master the Spanish language.) Had he lived longer his old association with Trotsky, Zinoviev and

Kamenev, his stubbornly defended heresies, and the offence he gave Stalin in 1923 would have counted against him; and he would hardly have avoided denunciation as an 'enemy of the people', a spy and a wrecker. But the great purges were still two or three years off, and so he was given a State funeral and was buried under the Heroes Wall at the Kremlin.

In the next twenty years bureaucratically ordained oblivion covered his person, his role in the revolution, his achievements and his writings. When Stalin's philosophical Inquisitors, Zhdanov or Alexandrov, mentioned him it was only to show him up as one who had strayed from the straight path of the true dogma. All the more intense has, in recent years, been the intelligentsia's curiosity for his ideas and personality. His work has been excavated slowly, laboriously and – selectively. The present ruling group finds it convenient to offer some of his writings, the more conventional ones or those touched already by the blight of Stalinism, to young and avid readers eager for access to the submerged intellectual heritage of the revolution. But Lunacharsky, the free and open mind, the erratic philosopher, the bold innovator, and last but not least, the brilliant actor and eye-witness of the revolution, is still an awkward embarrassment to officialdom; and so they still censor or hide carefully those of his writings – and there are many – in which they sense 'dynamite'.

This slim volume of profiles belongs, of course, to the explosives. A glance at its Table of Contents will explain why: most of the people, to whom Lunacharsky here pays his tributes are still 'unpersons' in the U.S.S.R. He pays his tributes in his own, warm-hearted and yet detached manner, portraying them in their strength and weakness alike. Even Lenin, who was already on his death-bed when Lunacharsky's Profile of him appeared, is not described here as the Saint-cum-Superman of the official legend. And Lunacharsky did not hesitate to portray Martov, the leader of the Mensheviks, with sympathy and pity; he even expressed the hope that Martov might yet find a place for himself within the Communist movement, as the leader of a 'right wing' in its ranks. How far all this was from the later 'monolithic' conception of the Party. The publishers of Allen Lane The Penguin Press have done well to commemorate Lunacharsky on the fiftieth anniversary of the revolution by bringing out this remarkable little volume of his. I hope that Lunacharsky's other writings will soon also be made available to the English reading public.

ISAAC DEUTSCHER

Harpur College
New York State
April 1967

A COMPARISON OF THE EDITIONS OF LUNACHARSKY'S 'SILHOUETTES'

The main text of this book is a translation of the 1923 edition of Lunacharsky's *Revolutionary Silhouettes* published by 'Transposektsiya' of Moscow, a trades-union publishing house, in an edition of 10,000 copies. The same work, or variants of it, was also published in three other editions before and after 1923.

The original version appeared in what was to have been the first book of a four-volume history of the October Revolution entitled *Velikii Perevorot* (*The Great Revolution*) published in Petrograd, 1919, by Grzhebin. At this time, two years after the revolution, private-enterprise publishing was still allowed. Grzhebin was a serious liberal publisher of the highest reputation and his 1919 non-fiction list contained, alongside Lunacharsky, memoirs and chronicles of the events of 1917 by authors from a relatively wide range of political allegiance: the Menshevik leaders Dan and Martov figure in it, Chernov the leader of the Right S.Rs, Potresov, Sukhanov and Liber, the *Bundist* leader. Numerous works of theology and non-Marxist philosophy also figure in the list. Soon afterwards Grzhebin emigrated to Berlin where he continued publishing in Russian well into the thirties. This move was made as much for purely practical reasons – shortage of paper and binding materials, labour problems – as on political grounds. In the early twenties not only were *émigré*-published books allowed into Soviet Russia with relative freedom but many official Soviet organizations wishing to distribute their books within Russia were actually obliged to have them published abroad, out of pressing economic and technical considerations. As a result of the disruption caused by the Civil War, the papermaking and printing industries – like the rest of the Russian economy – were in a very bad state.

This is the background to Lunacharsky's remarks in

his Foreword to the 1923 edition, in which he finds it necessary to explain his choice of Grzhebin as a publisher in 1919. He also complains that Grzhebin rushed the book into print without his knowledge and was continuing to publish it abroad 'without my permission'. These protestations should be taken with a pinch of salt. It is most improbable that the publication of *The Great Revolution* took place without his knowledge and even in 1923 there was nothing unusual in having one's books appearing under the imprint of such a respected *émigré* publisher as Grzhebin. It is much more likely that Lunacharsky had offended some highly-placed Party colleagues, perhaps by being too frank in his political autobiography which forms the longest chapter of the 1919 book, perhaps by not only omitting a profile of Stalin but even failing to make any more than one passing reference to him in the whole book.

In the enlarged and rewritten 1923 edition Lunacharsky cut out his political autobiography (which leads one to suspect that this was the offending portion in the 1919 edition), cut out a short profile of Kamenev and from various sources (listed in the Foreword) added his profiles of Plekhanov, Sverdlov, Volodarsky, Uritsky, F. I. Kalinin and Bessalko. Still not a mention of Stalin.

The next version, published in Kiev by the Ukrainian State Publishing House in 1924, is similar in content to the 1923 edition. The only differences are purely editorial: the style has been polished up, punctuation altered here and there, misprints corrected. After that this book never again saw the light of day in a complete form. It is reasonable to assume that Stalin took care of that.

In 1965, however, a very much truncated version was included in a volume of Lunacharsky's selected biographical works, in the series 'The Lives of Remarkable People' published by 'Young Guard', the Komsomol Publishing House in Moscow. This selection was compiled by Lunacharsky's daughter Irina and edited by I. Satz. Textually based on the 1924 edition, it omits the profiles of Trotsky, Zinoviev, Martov, F. I. Kalinin and Bessalko. The first three were obviously dropped because they are still 'unpersons'; F. I. Kalinin and Bessalko probably do not figure because they are both so deservedly obscure as to be of no interest in a volume intended for a young, non-specialist readership. The texts of those profiles which have been retained are significantly cut. To make the differences clear, a comparative table of contents of the four editions is given below:

1919	1923	1924	1965
Introduction	Foreword	Foreword	
My Party History			
Lenin	Lenin	Lenin	Lenin
Trotsky	Trotsky	Trotsky	
Zinoviev	Zinoviev	Zinoviev	
	Plekhanov	Plekhanov	Plekhanov
	Sverdlov	Sverdlov	Sverdlov
	Volodarsky	Volodarsky	Volodarsky
	Uritsky	Uritsky	Uritsky
Martov	Martov	Martov	
	F. I. Kalinin	F. I. Kalinin	
	Bessalko	Bessalko	
Kamenev			

The 1965 edition does not contain any interpolations into the 1924 text, but the editor does state that it 'is published . . . with minor omissions and with corrections of obvious mistakes'. This is nothing more than a euphemism for *suppressio veri*. Some of the cuts are marked thus: (. . .). Others are not indicated at all. The minor stylistic variations between the 1923 and 1924 texts do not affect the sense and are not worth recording.

The cuts in the 1924 text made in the 1965 edition are of two sorts: those referring to tabu figures such as Trotsky and Zinoviev, and those which mention Lenin in terms of anything less than total admiration. As a result Lunacharsky's profile of Lenin in the 1965 edition reads as flatly and uncritically as any other hack piece of Leninist hagiography, robbed of those mild hints about Lenin's inadequacies and errors which give Lunacharsky's account of the Bolshevik leader a degree, rare in Soviet writing, of humanity and credibility.

M. G.

REVOLUTIONARY
SILHOUETTES

FOREWORD

32

The present book is made up of a series of articles written on various occasions about some of our comrades in the R.C.P.

I should begin with a warning that these are not biographies, not testimonials, not portraits but merely profiles: it is their virtue and at the same time their limitation that they are entirely based on personal recollections.

In 1919 the publisher Grzhebin, whom I already knew and who had been recommended to me by Maxim Gorky, asked me to start writing my memoirs of the great revolution. I was soon able to deliver him the first – or more precisely the preliminary – volume, in which I attempted to acquaint the readers both with myself, as a point of reference in judging the rather more subjective aspects of my 'chronicle', and with the main *dramatis personae* of the revolution in so far as I knew them and in so far as a knowledge of their characters and the events of their pre-revolutionary lives seemed to me to merit further exposition.

That book, however, was overtaken by a strange fate. At a moment when circumstances precluded me from working on it and when I had become convinced that to write memoirs at a time when not a single event of the revolution had cooled down – we were still living in its very crucible – was simply impossible (Sukhanov's multi-volume work on the revolution, among others, had already convinced me of this); at a time, as it seemed to me, when any premature description of those events without an adequate study of the documents would be too subjective and little more than essay-writing – it was then that Grzhebin, unknown to me, published the first volume of my proposed memoirs. He is apparently continuing to publish them abroad, entirely without my permission.

I think it essential to state these facts here, in order to avoid any misunderstanding about the nature of that book.

I have now decided to extract from it, in slightly re-edited form, my character-sketches of comrades Lenin, Trotsky and Zinoviev. I still think that these profiles are quite accurate and fair and that some people may find them useful, in particular young members of the R.C.P. or sympathizers outside the framework of the Party.

The chief inadequacy of these profiles is their exclusive reliance on material that predates 1917. I also apologize for the fact that in one or two places I have been obliged *en passant* to talk about myself.

I have lengthened the essay on comrade Zinoviev.

I have added to these main essays a profile of Martov, also taken from my book *The Great Revolution*, and my obituaries of Uritsky, Kalinin and Bessalko, and I have rewritten my short memoirs of Volodarsky and Sverdlov since my previous writings on them have been mislaid.

My cursory recollections of G. V. Plekhanov were written at the request of the editor of the journal *Under The Banner of Marxism*, in which they were first published earlier this year.

A. LUNACHARSKY

Moscow, 20.III.23.

VLADIMIR ILYICH LENIN

I shall make no attempt here to write yet another biography of Lenin; for that there is no lack of other sources. I shall only refer to what I know of him from our personal relations and to my own direct impressions of the man.

I first heard of Lenin from Axelrod[1] after the publication of a book[2] written by 'Tulin'.[3] I had not yet read the book, but Axelrod said to me: 'Now we can really say that there is a genuine social-democratic movement in Russia and that real social-democratic thinkers are beginning to emerge.'

'What do you mean?' I enquired. 'What about Struve,[4] what about Tugan-Baranovsky?'[5] Axelrod gave a somewhat enigmatic smile (the fact is that he had once expressed the highest opinion of Struve) and said: 'Yes, but Struve and Tugan-Baranovsky – all that is just so many pages of donnish theorizing, so much historical data on the evolution of the Russian academic intelligentsia; Tulin on the other hand is a product of the Russian workers' movement, he is already a page in the history of the Russian revolution.'

Naturally Tulin's book was read abroad (I was in Zürich at the time) with the utmost avidity and was subjected to every form of comment. After that I heard no more than rumours of his arrest and exile at Krasnoyarsk[6] with Martov[7] and Potresov.[8] Lenin, Martov and Potresov appeared to be absolutely inseparable personal friends; they blended into a collective image of the purely Russian leadership of the newly-formed workers' movement. How strange it is now to see what different paths these 'three friends' were to follow!

The next book to reach us was *On the Development of Capitalism in Russia*.[9] Although personally less concerned with purely economic questions – I already regarded the characteristics and development of capitalism in Russia as incontestable – I was nevertheless amazed by the enormously solid statistical foundation of the book and the skill of its argumentation. It seemed to me at the time (as was indeed to be the case) that this book would give the death-blow to all the misconceived notions of Populist (*Narodnik*)[10] ideology.

I was in exile when news of the 2nd Congress[11] began to reach us. This was the time when *Iskra*[12] had begun publication and was already consolidating its position. I had unhesitatingly declared myself a supporter of *Iskra*, but I knew little of its contents because although we did get all the issues, they reached us at very irregular intervals. We nevertheless had the impression that the inseparable trio – Lenin, Martov and Potresov – had become indissolubly fused with the *émigré* trinity of Plekhanov,[13] Axelrod and Zasulich.[14] At all events the news of the split at the 2nd Congress hit us like a bolt from the blue. We knew that the 2nd Congress was to witness the concluding moves in the struggle with 'The Workers' Cause',[15] but that the schism should take a course which was to put Martov and Lenin in opposing camps and that Plekhanov was to 'split off' midway between the two – none of this so much as entered our heads.

The first clause of the Party statute – was this really something which justified a split?[16] A reshuffle of jobs on the editorial board – what's the matter with those people abroad, have they gone mad? We were disturbed more than anything else by this split and tried, from the meagre information which filtered through to us, to unravel what on earth was going on. There was no lack of rumours that Lenin was a trouble-maker and a splitter, that he wanted to set himself up as the autocrat of the Party at all costs, that Martov and Axelrod had refused, as it were, to swear fealty to him as the Grand Cham of the Party. This interpretation was, however, largely contradicted by the stand taken by Plekhanov, whose initial attitude, as we know, was one of close and friendly alliance with Lenin. It was not long before Plekhanov deserted to the Menshevik side, but all of us in exile (and not only those exiled in Vologda,[17]

I suspect) took this as being very much to Georgii Valentinovich's discredit. We Marxists had nothing to gain by such rapid changes of position.

In short, we were somewhat in the dark. I should add that the comrades in Russia who supported Lenin were also rather vague about what was happening. If we are to mention personalities, it was undoubtedly A. A. Bogdanov[18] who gave him the most powerful support. It was here that Bogdanov's adherence to Lenin was, I think, of decisive significance. If he had not sided with Lenin things would probably have progressed a great deal more slowly.

But why did Bogdanov associate himself with Lenin? He saw the quarrel which had broken out at the Congress as primarily a question of discipline: once a majority (even if only of one) had voted for Lenin's formulae, the minority should have acquiesced; secondly he saw it as a clash between the Russian section of the Party and the *émigrés*. Even though Lenin did not have a single big name on his side he did have, practically to a man, all the delegates who had come from Russia, whereas as soon as Plekhanov crossed the floor all the big *émigré* names were gathered in the Menshevik camp.

Bogdanov recalled the scene, although not quite accurately, as follows: the *émigré* aristocrats of the Party had refused to realize that we were now a real party and that what counted above all was the collective will of those who were doing the practical work in Russia. There is no doubt that this line, which gave rise, *inter alia*, to the slogan: 'A single Party centre – and in Russia', had a flattering and encouraging effect on many Party committees in Russia, which were by then spread in a fairly wide network throughout the country.

It soon became clear what sort of people were drawn to each of the two factions: the Mensheviks attracted the majority of the Marxist intellectuals in the capitals; they also had an undoubted success among the more skilled working men; the chief adherents of the Bolsheviks were in fact the committee members, i.e. the provincial Party workers, revolutionary professionals. These were largely made up of intellectuals of an obviously different type – not academic Marxist professors and students but people who had committed themselves irrevocably to their profession – revolution. It was largely this element to which Lenin attached such enormous significance and which he called 'the bacteria of revolution'; it was this section which was consolidated by Bogdanov, with the active support of the young Kamenev[19] and others, into the famous Organizational Bureau of Committees of the Majority and which was to supply Lenin with his army.

Bogdanov by then had served his term of exile and was spending some time abroad. I was absolutely convinced that he must have made a reasonably correct assessment of the problems and therefore, partly out of confidence in him, I also took up a pro-Bolshevik position.

My exile over, I managed to see comrade Krizhanovsky[20] in Kiev; he at the time was playing a fairly big part in affairs and was a close friend of comrade Lenin, although he was wavering between the strictly Leninist position and one of conciliationism. It was he who gave me a more detailed account of Lenin. He described him with enthusiasm, dwelling on his enormous intellect and inhuman energy; he described him as exceptionally kind and a magnificent friend, but he also remarked that Lenin was above all a political creature, that if he broke with somebody politically he would at once break off personal relations with him as well. Lenin was, in Krizhanovsky's words, merciless and undeviating in the struggle. Just as I was beginning to build up a fairly romantic image of the man in my mind's eye, Krizhanovsky added: 'And to look at he's like a well-heeled peasant from Yaroslavl, a cunning little *muzhik*, especially when he's wearing a beard.'

Hardly had I returned to Kiev from exile when I received a direct order from the Bureau of Committee of the Majority to go abroad immediately and join the editorial staff of the central organ of the Party.[21] This I did. I spent several months in Paris, partly because I wanted to make a closer study of the causes of the Party split. However, once in Paris I immediately found myself at the head of the very small local Bolshevik group and was soon involved in fighting the Mensheviks. Lenin wrote me a couple of short letters, in which he urged me to hurry to Geneva. In the end it was he who came to Paris.

To me his arrival was somewhat unexpected. He did not make a very good impression on me at first sight. His appearance struck me as somehow faintly colourless and he said nothing very definite apart from insisting on my immediate departure for Geneva.

I agreed to go.

At the same time Lenin decided to deliver a major lecture in Paris on the subject of the prospects of the Russian revolution and the fate of the Russian peasantry. It was at this lecture that I first heard him as an orator. Lenin was transformed. I was deeply impressed by that concentrated energy with which he spoke, by those piercing eyes of his which grew almost sombre as they bored gimlet-like into the audience, by the orator's monotonous but compelling movements, by that fluent diction so redolent of will-power. I realized that as a tribune this man was destined to make a powerful and ineradicable mark. And I already knew the extent of Lenin's strength as a publicist – his unpolished but extraordinarily clear style, his ability to present any idea, however complicated, in astonishingly simple form and to modify it in such a way that it would ultimately be engraved upon any mind, however dull and however unaccustomed to political thinking.

Only later, much later, did I come to see that Lenin's greatest gifts were not those of a tribune or a publicist, not even those of a thinker, but even in those early days it was obvious to me that the dominating trait of his character, the feature which constituted half his make-up, was his will: an extremely firm, extremely forceful will capable of concentrating itself on the most immediate task but which yet never strayed beyond the radius traced out by his powerful intellect and which assigned every individual problem its place as a link in a huge, world-wide political chain.

I think it was on the day after the lecture that we, for I

forget what reason, called on the sculptor Aronson,[22] with whom I was then on quite friendly terms. Catching sight of Lenin's head Aronson was enraptured and begged Lenin to allow him at least to sculpt a medallion of his head. He pointed out to me the amazing resemblance between Lenin and Socrates. I should add, incidentally, that Lenin bore a much closer likeness to Verlaine than to Socrates. An engraving of Carrière's[23] portrait of Verlaine had recently been published and a famous bust of Verlaine was on exhibition at the time, later to be bought by the Geneva museum. People had, in fact, remarked on Verlaine's unusual resemblance to Socrates, the chief similarity being in the magnificent shape of his head. The structure of Vladimir Ilyich's skull is truly striking. One has to study him for a little while and then instead of the first impression of a plain, large, bald head one begins to appreciate the physical power, the outlines of the colossal dome of his forehead, and to sense something which I can only describe as a physical emanation of light from its surface.

The sculptor, of course, noticed it at once.

Beside this, a feature which gave him more in common with Verlaine than with Socrates was his pair of small, deep-set and terrifyingly piercing eyes. But whereas in the great poet these eyes were sombre and rather lack-lustre (judging by Carrière's portrait), with Lenin they are mocking, full of irony, glittering with intelligence and a kind of teasing mirth. Only when he speaks do they become sombre and literally hypnotic. Lenin has very small eyes but they are so expressive, so inspired that later I was often to find myself admiring their spontaneous vivacity.

The eyes of Socrates, to judge by the busts of him, were rather more protuberant.

In the lower part of the head there is a further significant resemblance, especially when Lenin's beard is more or less fully grown. With Socrates, Verlaine and Lenin the beard grows in a similar way, slightly jutting and untidy. With all three the lower region of the face is somewhat shapeless, as if flung together as an afterthought.

A big nose and thick lips give Lenin something of a

Tartar look, which in Russia is of course easily explicable. But exactly the same or nearly the same nose and lips are to be found in Socrates, a fact particularly noticeable in Greece where a similar cast of features was usually only attributed to satyrs. It is the same with Verlaine. One of Verlaine's close friends nicknamed him 'The Kalmuck'. In the busts of the great philosopher, Socrates' countenance chiefly bears the stamp of deep thought. I believe, however, that if there is a grain of truth in the descriptions of him left by Xenophon and Plato, Socrates must have been a man of wit and irony and that in the lively play of his features there would, I submit, have been an even greater likeness to those of Lenin than the bust shows. Equally there predominates in both the famous portraits of Verlaine that mood of melancholy, that minor-key air of decadence which of course dominated his poetry; everyone knows, however, that Verlaine, especially in the early stages of his drunken spells, was a man of gay and ironic temper and I believe that here again the likeness was more than is apparent.

What is there to be learned from this strange parallel between a Greek philosopher, a great French poet and a great Russian revolutionary? The answer is, of course – nothing. If it indicates anything at all, then it simply shows that similar features may indeed be found in men who are perhaps of an equal rank of genius but of a totally different cast of mind; apart from that it provided me with a chance of describing Lenin's appearance in more or less graphic terms.

When I came to know Lenin better, I appreciated yet another side of him which is not immediately obvious – his astonishing vitality. Life bubbles and sparkles within him. Today, as I write these lines, Lenin is already fifty, yet he is still a young man, the whole tone of his life is youthful. How infectiously, how charmingly, with what childlike ease he laughs, how easy it is to amuse him, how prone he is to laughter, that expression of man's victory over difficulties! In the worst moments that he and I lived through together, Lenin was unshakeably calm and as ready as ever to break into cheerful laughter.

There was even something unusually endearing about his anger. Despite the fact that of late his displeasure might destroy dozens, perhaps even hundreds of people, he was always in control of his anger and it was expressed in almost joking manner. It was like a thunderstorm 'that seemed to sport and play, to rumble in a clear blue sky'. I have often noticed that alongside that outward seething, those angry words, those shafts of venomous irony there was a chuckle in his glance and the instant ability to put an end to the angry scene which he had apparently whipped up because it suited his purpose. Inwardly he remains not only calm but cheerful.

In his private life, too, Lenin loves the sort of fun which is unassuming, direct, simple and rumbustious. His favourites are children and cats; sometimes he can play with them for hours on end. Lenin also brings the same wholesome, life-enhancing quality to his work. I cannot say from personal experience that Lenin is hard-working; as it happens I have never seen him immersed in a book or bent over his desk. He writes his articles without the least effort and in a single draft free of all mistakes or revisions. He can do this at any moment of the day, usually in the morning after getting up, but he can do it equally well in the evening when he has returned from an exhausting day, or at any other time. Recently his reading, with the possible exception of a short interval spent abroad during the period of reaction, has been fragmentary rather than extensive, but from every book, from every single page that he reads Lenin draws something new, stores away some essential idea which he will later employ as a weapon. He is not particularly stimulated by ideas that are cognate with his own thought, but rather by those that conflict with his. The ardent polemicist is always alive in him.

But if there is something slightly ridiculous in calling Lenin industrious, he is on the other hand capable of enormous effort when required. I would almost be prepared to say that he is absolutely tireless; if that is not strictly so it is because I know that the inhuman efforts which he has lately been forced to make have caused his powers to flag somewhat towards the end of each week and have obliged him to rest.*

But then Lenin is one of those people who knows how to relax. He takes his rest like taking a bath and when he does so he stops thinking about anything; he completely gives himself up to idleness and whenever possible to his favourite amusement and to laughter. In this way Lenin emerges from the briefest spell of rest freshened and ready for the fray again.

It is this well-spring of sparkling and somehow naïve vitality which, together with the solid breadth of his intellect and his intense will-power, constitutes Lenin's fascination. This fascination is colossal: people who come close to his orbit not only become devoted to him as a political leader but in some odd way they fall in love with him. This applies to people of the most varying calibre and cast of mind, ranging from such enormously sensitive and gifted men as Gorky to a lumpish peasant from the depths of the country, from a first-class political brain like Zinoviev to some soldier or sailor who only yesterday belonged to the Jew-baiting 'Black Hundred' gangs[24] who now is prepared to risk his tousled head for the 'leader of the world revolution – Ilyich'. This familiar form of his name, Ilyich, has become so widespread that it is used by people who have never seen Lenin.

When Lenin lay wounded – mortally, we feared – no one expressed our feelings about him better than Trotsky. Amidst the appalling turmoil of world events it was Trotsky, the other leader of the Russian revolution, a man by no means inclined to sentimentality, who said: 'When you realize that Lenin might die it seems that all our lives are useless and you lose the will to live.'

To return to the thread of my recollections of Lenin before the great revolution: in Geneva Lenin and I worked together on the editorial board of the journal *Forward*, then on *The Proletarian*. Lenin was a good man to work

* On re-reading these lines now, in March 1923, when Lenin is gravely ill, I am bound to admit that neither we nor he himself took enough care of him. Nevertheless I am convinced that Vladimir Ilyich's herculean constitution will overcome his illness and that before long he will return to the leadership of the R.C.P. and of Russia.

with as an editor. He wrote a lot and he wrote easily, as I have already mentioned, and took a very conscientious attitude towards his colleagues' work: he frequently corrected them, gave advice and was delighted by any talented and convincing article.

In the first period of our life in Geneva up to January 1905 we spent most of our time on internal Party quarrels. Here I was astonished by Lenin's profound indifference to every form of polemical skirmishing. He set very little store by the struggle to capture the *émigré* readership, which largely supported the Mensheviks. He failed to attend a number of solemn discussion meetings and made no effort to suggest that I should go to them either. He preferred me to spend my time on writing full-length papers and essays.

In his attitude to his enemies there was no feeling of bitterness, but nevertheless he was a cruel political opponent, exploiting any blunder they made and exaggerating every hint of opportunism – in which by the way he was quite correct, because later the Mensheviks themselves were to fan their erstwhile sparks into a sizeable blaze of opportunism. He never dabbled in intrigue, although in the political struggle he deployed every weapon except dirty ones. The Mensheviks, I should point out, behaved in exactly the same way. Relations between the factions were in any event pretty bad and there were not many of those who were political opponents at that time who were able to maintain any sort of normal personal relations. For us the Mensheviks had become enemies. Dan, in particular,[25] poisoned the Mensheviks' attitude towards us. Lenin had always disliked Dan, whereas he had always liked Martov and still does,* but he always regarded him and still regards him as politically spineless and prone to lose sight of the main objectives in his fine-spun political theorizing.

With the forward march of revolutionary events, matters changed considerably. Firstly we began to gain something like a moral superiority over the Mensheviks.

* On the day that I was reading the final proof of this 'profile' there came the news of Martov's death.

It was then that the Mensheviks turned firmly to the slogan: push the bourgeoisie forward and strive for a constitution or at the best for a democratic republic. Our attitude of being technicians of revolution, as the Mensheviks claimed, was attracting a significant proportion of *émigré* opinion, in particular that of young people. We could feel firm ground under our feet. Lenin in those days was magnificent. With the utmost enthusiasm he unfolded a prospect of merciless revolutionary struggle to come, and set off in a passion for Russia.[26]

At this point I went to Italy, due to poor health and fatigue, and I only kept in touch with Lenin by a correspondence that was largely concerned with matters of practical policy concerning our newspaper.

I next met him in Petersburg. I am bound to say that this period of Lenin's activity, in 1905 and 1906, seems to me to have been a comparatively ineffective one. Of course, even then he wrote a considerable number of brilliant articles and remained the leader of what was politically the most active of the parties – the Bolsheviks. I watched him closely throughout that period, because it was then that I had begun to make a close study from good sources of the lives of Cromwell and Danton. In trying to analyse the psychology of revolutionary 'leaders', I compared Lenin with figures such as these and I wondered whether Lenin really was such a genuinely revolutionary leader as he had seemed to be. I began to feel that life as an *émigré* had somewhat reduced Lenin's stature, that for him the internal party struggle with the Mensheviks had overshadowed the much greater struggle against the monarchy and that he was more of a journalist than a real leader.

It was bitter news to hear that discussions with the Mensheviks, to define the precise bounds between the two factions, were even going on whilst Moscow was prostrate from the effects of an unsuccessful armed uprising. Furthermore Lenin, from fear of arrest, made only rare appearances as a speaker; as far as I remember he did so on only one occasion, under the pseudonym of Karpov. He was recognized and given a magnificent ovation. He worked chiefly behind the scenes, almost exclusively with his pen and at various committee meetings of local Party branches. In short, Lenin, I felt, was still carrying on the fight rather on the old *émigré* scale, without expanding the work to the more grandiose proportions which the revolution was then assuming. Nevertheless I still regarded him as the leading political figure in Russia and I began to fear that the revolution lacked a real leader of genius.

To talk of Nosar-Khrustalev[27] was, of course, ridiculous. We all realized that this 'leader' who had so suddenly emerged had no future at all. A great deal more noise and glitter surrounded Trotsky, but at that time we all regarded Trotsky as a very able if somewhat theatrical tribune and not as a politician of the first rank. Dan and Martov were making extraordinary efforts to carry on the fight in the very heart of the Petersburg working class and as always they directed it against us, the Bolsheviks.

I now think that the 1905–6 revolution caught us somewhat unprepared and that we lacked real political skill. It was our later work in the Duma, our later work as *émigrés* in turning ourselves into practical politicians, in dealing with the problems of genuinely national politics, to which we were more or less convinced we should return sooner or later – it was this that added to our inner stature, which completely altered our manner of approach to the question of revolution when history summoned us again. This is especially true of Lenin.

I did not see Lenin while he was in Finland,[28] when he was in hiding from the forces of reaction. I next met him abroad, at the Stuttgart congress.[29] Here he and I were particularly close, quite apart from the fact that we were constantly conferring together as a result of the Party having entrusted me with one of the most essential jobs at the Congress. We had a number of major political discussions more or less in private, in which we weighed up the prospects of the great social revolution. On this subject Lenin was generally more of an optimist than I was. I considered that events would develop rather slowly, that we should obviously have to wait until capitalism was established in the Asian countries, that capitalism still had quite a few shots in its locker and that we might not see a true social revolution until our old age. This outlook genuinely upset Lenin. When I set out to prove my case to him I noticed a real shadow of sorrow crossing his powerful, intelligent features and I realized how passionately this man wanted not only to see the revolution in his lifetime but to exert himself in creating it. However, although he refused to agree with me he was obviously prepared to make a realistic admission that it would be an uphill task and to act accordingly.

Lenin turned out to possess the greater political insight, which is not surprising. He has the ability to raise opportunism to the level of genius, by which I mean the kind of opportunism which can seize on the precise moment and which always knows how to exploit it for the unvarying objective of the revolution. While Lenin was engaged on his great work during the Russian revolution he showed some remarkable examples of this brilliant timing, and he spelled this out in his last speech at the 4th Congress of the Third International,[30] a speech uniquely interesting in subject-matter and in which he described what one might call the philosophy of the tactics of retreat. Both Danton and Cromwell had this same ability.

I should add in passing that Lenin was always very shy and inclined to lurk in the shadows at international congresses, perhaps because he lacked confidence in his knowledge of languages – although he speaks good German and has no mean grasp of French and English. In spite of this he used to limit his public utterances at congresses to a few sentences. This has changed since Lenin has felt himself, at first hesitantly and then unconditionally, to be the leader of world revolution. As long ago as Zimmerwald and Kienthal,[31] where I was not present, Lenin appears, along with Zinoviev, to have made a number of major speeches in foreign languages. At the congresses of the Third International he frequently made long speeches which he refused to have translated by interpreters but instead generally made the speech himself first in German and then in French. He always spoke them with complete fluency and expressed his thoughts clearly and concisely. I was therefore all the more touched by a small document which I recently saw among the exhibits of the 'Red Moscow' museum. It was a questionnaire, filled out in Vladimir Ilyich's own hand. Opposite the question 'Have you a fluent spoken knowledge of any foreign language?' Ilyich had firmly written: 'None.' A trifle, but one which perfectly illustrates his unusual modesty. It will be appreciated by anybody who has witnessed the tremendous ovations which the Germans, the French and other western Europeans have given Lenin after he has made speeches in foreign languages.

I am very glad that I was never personally involved in our lengthy political quarrel with Lenin. I refer to the episode when Bogdanov, myself and others adopted a leftist deviation and formed the *Forward*[32] group, in which we mistakenly disagreed with Lenin in his appraisal of the Party's need to exploit the possibilities of legal political action during Stolypin's reactionary ministry.

During that period of disagreement Lenin and I never met. I was very much disturbed by Lenin's political ruthlessness when it was directed against us. I now believe that much of what divided the Bolsheviks and the Forwardists was simply a product of the misunderstandings and irritations of *émigré* life, quite apart, of course, from our very serious differences of opinion on philosophical matters; there was, after all, no reason for a political split between us because we both only represented shades of one and the same political viewpoint. At the time Bogdanov was so annoyed that he predicted that Lenin would inevitably leave the revolutionary movement and even tried to prove to comrade E. K. Malinovskaya[32] and to myself that Lenin was bound to end up as an Octobrist.[33]

Yes, Lenin certainly became an Octobrist – but what a different October that was!

I should like to add the following to these cursory remarks: I have often had to collaborate with Lenin on drafting resolutions of all kinds. This was generally done collectively – Lenin liked cooperative work on such occasions. Recently I was called upon to undertake similar work on drafting the resolution for the 8th Congress[35] on the peasant question.

Lenin himself is always extremely resourceful on such occasions; he quickly finds the appropriate words and phrases, weighs them up from every angle, sometimes rejects them. He is always very glad of help from any quarter. When someone manages to hit on exactly the right phrasing – 'That's it, that's it, well said, dictate that', Lenin will say in such cases. If he thinks some words are doubtful he will stare into space, ponder and say: 'I think it would sound better like this.' Sometimes, having laughingly accepted some critical objection, he will alter the wording that he himself has just put forward in all confidence.

Under Lenin's chairmanship this kind of work always proceeds extraordinarily quickly and somehow cheerfully. Not only does his own mind function at the top of its bent; he stimulates the minds of others to the highest degree.

I shall add nothing more at present to these recollections of mine, which largely make up my impressions of Vladimir Ilyich in the period before the 1917 revolution. Naturally I have a wealth of impressions and views concerning his absolute genius in the leadership of the Russian and world revolution, which was our leader's contribution to history.

I have not given up the idea of writing a more exhaustive political portrait of Vladimir Ilyich on the basis of that experience. There is, of course, a whole series of new characteristics which have enriched my view of him during these last six years of our work together, none of which, be it said, contradict those I have singled out, but which constitute further first-hand evidence of his personality. But the time is yet to come for drawing such a broad and comprehensive portrait.

Those comrades who may wish to re-publish these pages from the first volume of *The Great Revolution* (to which I have made only slight editorial emendations) will not, I feel, be mistaken in the belief that my work, too, has its place of some small value in the history of Russia and of the modern world, which in our country has always rightfully attracted such a keen interest among the very widest circles.

NOTES

Lunacharsky's original profile of Lenin was written in 1918 and published in 1919. Rather than attempt to summarize the numerous studies of Lenin's activities up to October 1917 it may be of value in this instance to sketch in the circumstances that followed the revolution. Lunacharsky was writing for people who were living in the immediate post-revolutionary turmoil, a time when Lenin had just begun to play a role which was the exact opposite of his previous function of would-be destroyer and usurper: he was now the head of an unstable, narrowly-based government of Russia which had suddenly inherited, in a magnified twentieth-century form, most of the accumulated problems which had bedevilled the country's past rulers. Brutus was now clad in Caesar's robe and inevitably not only his fellow-conspirators but the on-stage crowd and the bewildered foreign audience saw him in a different light.

In late 1917 and 1918 Lenin's new-born Bolshevik regime was threatened from within and without. First and above all loomed the stark, unavoidable fact that revolutionary Russia was on the point of total military defeat by imperial Germany. Yet despite Russia's war-weariness, the thought of capitulation evoked a violently 'patriotic' reaction in politicians and masses alike. For reasons in which emotion and calculation were inextricably mixed, the dominant mood of the country was for fighting on and in a stormy meeting of Bolshevik leaders on 8 January 1918 Lenin was voted down by an absolute majority for continuing the war. Unaffected by his colleagues' illusions, Lenin temporized, manoeuvred and pressed for peace. He was helped by the Germans, who terrified the Bolsheviks by resuming their advance into Russia on 17 February. Under threat of Lenin's resignation his peace policy scraped through the Central Committee on 23 February, and on 3 March 1918 the treaty of Brest-Litovsk was signed. Russia lost Finland, the Ukraine, the Baltic states, eastern Poland and a large slice of Caucasian territory; but the heartland of Russia was saved for the Revolution,

Germany turned westward to deal with the Allies and was herself crushed eight months later. Lenin had shown that he was a Russian statesman of international calibre. At the time hardly anyone was capable of realizing this: at home the 'Left Communists' shrilly accused him of betraying the Revolution whilst abroad *The Times* had summed up official western opinion by growling: 'They [the Allies] know that the Maximalists [Bolsheviks] are a band of anarchists and fanatics who have seized power for the moment, owing to the paralysis of national life. . . . They know that Lenin and several of his confederates are adventurers of German-Jewish blood and in German pay . . .'

In the breathing-space won at Brest-Litovsk internal problems now beset Lenin with equal force. The economy was in ruins and hunger threatened the cities. The dissolution of society and the undermining of respect for authority of any sort were proving a serious embarrassment now that the Bolsheviks had to act constructively. Both the Left S.Rs and the 'Left Communists' within the Bolshevik ranks were making potentially dangerous trouble. The latter were probably the least of Lenin's difficulties. With his long experience of dealing with Party *frondeurs* he knew that provided they were allowed to go on talking their heads off whilst being excluded from influence on the really vital issues, they could be both neutralized and harnessed to vital but secondary tasks; Lunacharsky himself, appointed to the Commissariat of Education, was a typical example of such skilful treatment. The Left S.Rs were harder to tame, because they were outside Lenin's immediate control. They delivered themselves into his hands, however, when they staged a revolt in July 1918 against the Brest-Litovsk treaty, assassinated Von Mirbach the German ambassador and capped it by assassinating Uritsky the following month; on the same day the nearly successful attempt on Lenin's own life, despite the lack of evidence to associate his assailant Fanny Kaplan with the S.Rs, proved the final excuse for letting loose an outburst of terror against the S.Rs and other anti-Bolsheviks of whatever ilk.

The ills of the Russian economy, by contrast, were less susceptible to cure by rifle-fire and it was in this sector that Lenin in 1918–19 achieved relatively little. For the moment threats, exhortation and improvisation were the only measures that the Bolsheviks seemed capable of taking and they were not enough. For nearly five years Russia lived from hand to mouth and it is amazing that Lenin's regime did not founder on the one problem which he failed to solve – bread.

Yet in the crucial matter of survival in the face of violent civil war, Lenin managed the apparently impossible. A year after 1917 – a time when officers were liable to be lynched and the armed forces were little more than a dangerously anarchic mob – a disciplined Red Army and Navy had been created which beat the White generals and their *Entente* backers to a standstill. All these facts should be borne in mind when reading Lunacharsky's gentle, admiring memoirs of Lenin before 1917, which give little hint of the ruthless strength of the man who rode the Russian tiger.

1. AXELROD: Pavel Borisovich Axelrod (1850–1928). Pseudonym of Pinkhas Boruch Axelrod. Early Marxist theoretician. One of the founders of the 'Liberation of Labour' group, 1883. Became Menshevik after 1903 Party split.

2. A BOOK: Refers to Lenin's work *The Economic Content of Populism and its Critique in Mr Struve's Book*, published in a collection of Marxist articles, St Petersburg, 1895.

3. 'TULIN': 'K. Tulin' was Lenin's first pseudonym, which he used between 1895 and 1900.

4. STRUVE: Pyotr Berngardovich Struve (1870–1944). One of the earliest Russian Marxist theorists. Although he drafted the first manifesto of the Russian Social Democratic Party in 1898, Struve changed his politics in 1902 and joined the liberal Kadet party (q.v. below p. 71). During Civil War, foreign minister of Wrangel's 'White' government in the Crimea. Died in Paris.

5. TUGAN-BARANOVSKY: Mikhail Ivanovich Tugan-Baranovsky (1865–1919). Economics professor at St Petersburg University. 'Legal' Marxist. In 1918 Minister of Finance in short-lived Ukrainian government of Hetman Skoropadsky.

6. KRASNOYARSK: Third largest town in Siberia, on upper reaches of River Yeneisei, southern central Siberia. From February 1897 Lenin spent first three months of his Siberian exile in Krasnoyarsk.

7. MARTOV: Yulii Osipovich Tsederbaum, alias Martov (1873–1923). See below pp. 131–40.

8. POTRESOV: Alexandr Nikolayevich Potresov (1869–1934). Early Russian socialist, collaborated with Lenin in

early days of Party journal *The Spark* (*Iskra*). Became right-wing Menshevik after 1905 revolution, but broke with Mensheviks after 1917 as being insufficiently vigorous in their opposition to Bolsheviks. Emigrated in 1927.

9. ON THE DEVELOPMENT OF CAPITALISM IN RUSSIA: Published St Petersburg, 1899.

10. NARODNIK: Name applied to the non-Marxist Russian agrarian socialist movement of the latter half of the nineteenth century. Based its theories of reform on the Russian peasants' system of communal land tenure. Employed terrorism as political weapon.

11. 2ND CONGRESS: 2nd Congress of Russian Social Democratic Workers' Party, held in Brussels and London, 1903, at which the split occurred dividing the party into Bolsheviks and Mensheviks.

12. ISKRA: *The Spark* – Party journal of the Russian Social Democrats, of which Lenin was member of the editorial board from December 1900 to October 1903.

13. PLEKHANOV: Georgii Valentinovich Plekhanov (1857–1918). See below pp. 85–100.

14. ZASULICH: Vera Ivanovna Zasulich (1851–1919). Began her political career as a Narodnik. She attempted, aged seventeen, to assassinate Trepov, military governor of St Petersburg. Was tried but acquitted and allowed to escape abroad. Became a Marxist in the early 1880s and was one of the first members of the Russian Social Democratic party.

15. 'THE WORKERS' CAUSE': First social democratic newspaper in Russia. From 1898 to 1903 represented the official grouping of the S.D. party in emigration. The 'struggle' referred to was between *The Workers' Cause* and *The Spark* for recognition as the official Party organ.

16. THE FIRST CLAUSE OF THE PARTY STATUTE: The wording of this clause, which defined Party membership, was one of the sharpest points of difference between Lenin and Martov in the split of the Russian Social Democratic party into the Bolshevik and Menshevik factions.

17. THOSE EXILED IN VOLOGDA: Refers to Lunacharsky himself, who was exiled to Vologda from 1900 to 1902. Vologda, a town in northern European Russia, is approximately halfway between Moscow and Archangel.

18. A. A. BOGDANOV: Alexandr Alexandrovich Malinovsky alias Bogdanov (1873–1928). Philosopher, sociologist, economist and surgeon. Joined the Social Democratic party in

1890s, became a Bolshevik at the Party split in 1903. Became leader of the left-wing Bolshevik 'Forward' group (q.v. below). Served in the First World War as an army doctor. After 1917, although then outside the Bolshevik party, was influential as a somewhat heterodox Communist ideologist and as theorist of the 'Proletarian Culture' movement (q.v. below). After 1923 devoted himself to medicine; died during an experiment on himself.

19. KAMENEV: Lev Borisovich Rosenfeld, alias Kamenev (1883–1936). Joined the Social Democratic party in 1901; a Bolshevik in 1903. Close associate of Lenin. Arrested and exiled to Siberia in November 1914. Released February 1917. Chairman, Central Executive Committee of Soviets. Supported Trotsky in the anti-Stalin opposition. 1926–27 Soviet Ambassador to Italy. Condemned and executed in the first major 'purge' trial, 1936.

20. KRZHIZHANOVSKY: Gleb Maximilianovich Krzhizhanovsky (1872– ?). Became Marxist in 1891. Graduated from St Petersburg as an engineer 1894. Early Bolshevik. In 1895 arrested and exiled to Siberia. Emigrated to Munich in 1901, collaborated on *Iskra*. Elected to Central Committee of S.D. Party at 2nd Congress, 1903. An organizer of the railway strike in the 1905 revolution. Member of Moscow Soviet during 1917. Originated the plan for the electrification of Russia. Founded and ran *Gosplan* (State Planning Commission) from 1921 to 1930. Vice-president, U.S.S.R. Academy of Sciences.

21. THE CENTRAL ORGAN OF THE PARTY: In 1904, in Geneva, Lunacharsky contributed editorially to the Bolshevik journal *Forward*; after the 3rd Congress of the Party in 1905 *Forward* was officially closed down and at once restarted, entitled *The Proletarian.* To call it 'the central organ of the Party' is a piece of sophistry; it was a Bolshevik factional journal.

22. THE SCULPTOR ARONSON: Naum Aronson. Born at Kieslavka, Ukraine. Russian-Jewish sculptor whose most famous work is the Beethoven monument at Bonn. Awarded gold medal at Liège, 1906. His bust of Lenin was exhibited at the Soviet pavilion at the 1937 World Fair in Paris.

23. CARRIÈRE'S PORTRAIT OF VERLAINE: Eugène Carrière (1849–1906). French painter and sculptor.

24. BLACK HUNDRED GANGS: Name given by their opponents to right-wing, proto-fascist extremist organizations

in early twentieth-century Russia. Made the first extensive use of the 'pogrom' as a form of organized anti-Semitic terror.

25. DAN IN PARTICULAR: Fyodor Ilyich Gurvich, alias Dan (1871–1947). Married to the sister of Martov. Joined Social Democratic party in 1894. Became Menshevik in 1903. Shared with Martov the leadership of the Menshevik faction until after October 1917. Later emigrated and died in New York.

26. SET OFF . . . FOR RUSSIA: Lenin reached St Petersburg on 21 November 1905.

27. NOSAR-KHRUSTALEV: Georgii Stepanovich Nosar-Khrustalev (1879–1919). (Sometimes referred to as 'Khrustalev-Nosar'.) First chairman of the St Petersburg Soviet of Workers' Deputies during the 1905 revolution. Became a Menshevik in 1907. Gave up politics, became a journalist in the right-wing Press. Headed the ephemeral 'Khrustalev Republic' in the Ukraine during the Civil War. Shot by the Bolsheviks.

28. FINLAND: To avoid the tsarist police, Lenin went to Finland in January 1907, where he spent four months at Kuokkala.

29. THE STUTTGART CONGRESS: Congress of the socialist Second International held in 1907.

30. 4TH CONGRESS OF THE THIRD INTERNATIONAL: Held 1922–3 in Moscow. The Third International was the Bolshevik-dominated Communist international movement, usually known as the 'Comintern', so called to distinguish it from the Second or 'socialist' International.

31. ZIMMERWALD AND KIENTHAL: In September 1915 certain socialists, including some Bolsheviks and Mensheviks from the Russian Party, dissenting from their fellow socialists who had supported their respective countries' military efforts in the war, organized an anti-war conference at Zimmerwald in Switzerland. Lenin participated and took up an extreme 'left' anti-war position. A second similar conference (called the 'Second Zimmerwald' conference) was held in April 1916 at Kienthal. Lenin's extremist attitude was strongly held and resulted in a manifesto urging the European working class to stop fighting each other and turn on their capitalist exploiters.

32. THE 'FORWARD' GROUP: Radical sub-faction of the Bolsheviks, founded by Bogdanov, Lunacharsky and Gorky in 1909. Ideologically inspired by Bogdanov, it disagreed with

Lenin on the tactics of participation in the Duma. The group soon lost political significance and Lunacharsky returned to orthodox Bolshevism in 1917.

33. E. K. MALINOVSKAYA: Wife of A. A. Bogdanov (Malinovsky). See above p. 53.

34. OCTOBRIST: Russian political party of right-wing liberals, formed in 1905, led by A. I. Guchkov and M. V. Rodzyanko. Title adopted from the Imperial Manifesto of 17 *October* 1905 granting a constitution.

35. 8TH CONGRESS: Congress of the Bolshevik Party held in March 1919. Its most important resolution decreed the separation of Party and Soviet organizations.

LEV DAVIDOVICH TROTSKY

Trotsky entered the history of our Party somewhat unexpectedly and with instant brilliance. As I have heard, he began his social-democratic activity on the school bench and he was exiled before he was eighteen.

He escaped from exile. He first caused comment when he appeared at the Second Party Congress, at which the split occurred. Trotsky evidently surprised people abroad by his eloquence, by his education, which was remarkable for a young man, and by his aplomb. An anecdote was told about him which is probably not true, but which is nevertheless characteristic, according to which Vera Ivanovna Zasulich, with her usual expansiveness, having met Trotsky, exclaimed in the presence of Plekhanov: 'That young man is undoubtedly a genius'; the story goes that as Plekhanov left the meeting he said to someone: 'I shall never forgive this of Trotsky.' It is a fact that Plekhanov did not love Trotsky, although I believe that it was not because the good Zasulich called him a genius but because Trotsky had attacked him during the 2nd Congress with unusual heat and in fairly uncomplimentary terms. Plekhanov at the time regarded himself as a figure of absolutely inviolable majesty in social-democratic circles; even outsiders who disagreed with him approached him with heads bared and such cheekiness on Trotsky's part was bound to infuriate him. The Trotsky of those days undoubtedly had a great deal of juvenile bumptiousness. If the truth be told, because of his youth nobody took him very seriously, but everybody admitted that he possessed remarkable talent as an orator and they sensed too, of course, that this was no chick but a young eagle.

I first met him at a comparatively late stage, in 1905, after the events of January.[1] He had arrived, I forget where from, in Geneva and he and I were due to speak at a big meeting summoned as a result of this catastrophe. Trotsky then was unusually elegant, unlike the rest of us, and very handsome. This elegance and his nonchalant, condescending manner of talking to people, no matter who they were, gave me an unpleasant shock. I regarded this young dandy with extreme dislike as he crossed his legs and pencilled some notes for the impromptu speech that he was to make at the meeting. But Trotsky spoke very well indeed.

He also spoke at an international meeting, where I spoke for the first time in French and he in German; we both found foreign languages something of an obstacle, but we somehow survived the ordeal. Then, I remember, we were nominated – I by the Bolsheviks, he by the Mensheviks – to some commission on the division of joint funds and there Trotsky adopted a distinctly curt and arrogant tone.

Until we returned to Russia after the first (1905) revolution I did not see him again, nor did I see much of him during the course of the 1905 revolution. He held himself apart not only from us but from the Mensheviks too. His work was largely carried out in the Soviet of Workers' Deputies and together with Parvus[2] he organized some kind of a separate group which published a very militant, very well-edited small and cheap newspaper.[3]

I remember someone saying in Lenin's presence: 'Khrustalev's star is waning and now the strong man in the Soviet is Trotsky.' Lenin's face darkened for a moment, then he said: 'Well, Trotsky has earned it by his brilliant and unflagging work.'

Of all the Mensheviks Trotsky was then the closest to us, but I do not remember him once taking part in the fairly lengthy discussions between us and the Mensheviks on the subject of reuniting. By the Stockholm congress[4] he had already been arrested.

His popularity among the Petersburg proletariat at the time of his arrest was tremendous and increased still more as a result of his picturesque and heroic behaviour in court. I must say that of all the social-democratic leaders of 1905–6 Trotsky undoubtedly showed himself, despite his youth, to be the best prepared. Less than any of them did he bear the stamp of a certain kind of *émigré* narrowness of outlook which, as I have said, even affected Lenin at that time. Trotsky understood better than all the others what it meant to conduct the political struggle on a broad, national scale. He emerged from the revolution having acquired an enormous degree of popularity, whereas neither Lenin nor Martov had effectively gained any at all. Plekhanov had lost a great deal, thanks to his display of quasi-Kadet[5] tendencies. Trotsky stood then in the very front rank.

During the second emigration Trotsky took up residence in Vienna and in consequence my encounters with him were rare.

At the international conference in Stuttgart he behaved unassumingly and called upon us to do the same, considering that we had been knocked out of the saddle by the reaction of 1906 and were therefore incapable of commanding the respect of the congress.

Subsequently Trotsky was attracted by the conciliationist line and by the idea of the unity of the Party. More than anyone else he bent his efforts to that end at various plenary sessions and he devoted two-thirds of the work of his Vienna newspaper *Pravda* and of his group to the completely hopeless task of re-uniting the Party.

The only successful result which he achieved was the plenum at which he threw the 'liquidators'[6] out of the Party, nearly expelled the 'Forwardists' and even managed for a time to stitch up the gap – though with extremely weak thread – between the Leninites and the Martovites. It was that Central Committee meeting which, among other things, despatched comrade Kamenev as Trotsky's general watchdog (Kamenev was, incidentally, Trotsky's brother-in-law) but such a violent rift developed between Kamenev and Trotsky that Kamenev very soon returned to Paris. I must say here and now that Trotsky was extremely bad at organizing not only the Party but even a small group of it. He had practically no whole-hearted supporters at all; if he succeeded in impressing himself on the Party, it was entirely by his personality. The fact that he was quite incapable of fitting into the ranks of the Mensheviks made them react to him as though he were a kind of social-democratic anarchist and his behaviour annoyed them greatly. There was no question, at that time, of his total identification with the Bolsheviks. Trotsky seemed to be closest to the Martovites and indeed he always acted as though he were.

His colossal arrogance and an inability or unwillingness to show any human kindness or to be attentive to people, the absence of that charm which always surrounded Lenin, condemned Trotsky to a certain loneliness. One only has to recall that even a number of his personal friends (I am speaking, of course, of the political sphere) turned into his sworn enemies; this happened, for instance, in the case of his chief lieutenant, Semkovsky,[7] and it occurred later with the man who was virtually his favourite disciple, Skobeliev.[8]

Trotsky had little talent for working within political bodies; however, in the great ocean of political events, where such personal traits were completely unimportant, Trotsky's entirely positive gifts came to the fore.

I next came together with Trotsky at the Copenhagen Congress.[9] On arrival Trotsky for some reason saw fit to publish an article in *Vorwärts*[10] in which, having indiscriminately run down the entire Russian delegation, he declared that in effect they represented nobody but a lot of *émigrés*. This infuriated both Mensheviks and Bolsheviks. Plekhanov, who could not stand Trotsky, seized the opportunity to arraign Trotsky before a kind of court. This seemed to me unjust and I spoke up fairly energetically for Trotsky, and I was instrumental (together with Ryazanov)[11] in ensuring that Plekhanov's plan came to nothing. . . . Partly for that reason, partly, perhaps more, by chance, Trotsky and I began to see more of each other during the congress: we took time off together, we talked a lot on many subjects, mainly political, and we parted on quite good terms.

Soon after the Copenhagen Congress we Forwardists organized our second party school in Bologna and invited

Trotsky to come and run our practical training in journalism and to deliver a course of lectures on, if I am not mistaken, the parliamentary tactics of the German and Austrian Social Democrats and on the history of the Social Democratic Party in Russia. Trotsky kindly agreed to this proposal and spent nearly a month in Bologna. It is true that he maintained his own political line the whole time and tried to dislodge our pupils from their extreme left viewpoint and steer them further towards a conciliatory and middle-of-the-road attitude – a position, incidentally, which he himself regarded as strongly leftist. Although this political game of his proved fruitless, our pupils greatly enjoyed his highly talented lectures and in general throughout his whole stay Trotsky was unusually cheerful; he was brilliant, he was extremely loyal towards us and he left the best possible impression of himself. He was one of the most outstanding workers at our second party school.

My final meetings with Trotsky were even more prolonged and more intimate. These took place in Paris in 1915. Trotsky joined the editorial board of *Our Word*,[12] which was naturally accompanied by the usual intrigues and unpleasantness: someone was frightened by his joining us, afraid that such a strong personality might take over the newspaper altogether. But this aspect of the affair was of minor importance. A much more acute matter was that of Trotsky's attitude to Martov. We sincerely wanted to bring about, on a new basis of internationalism, the complete unification of our Party front all the way from Lenin to Martov. I spoke up for this course in the most energetic fashion and was to some degree the originator of the slogan 'Down with the "defeatists",[13] long live the unity of all Internationalists!'[14] Trotsky fully associated himself with this. It had long been his dream and it seemed to justify his whole past attitude.

We had no disagreements with the Bolsheviks, but with the Mensheviks things were going badly. Trotsky tried by every means to persuade Martov to break his links with the Defencists. The meetings of the editorial board turned into lengthy discussions, during which Martov, with astounding mental agility, almost with a kind of cunning sophistry, avoided a direct answer to the question whether he would break with the Defencists,[15] and at times Trotsky attacked him extremely angrily. Matters reached the point of an almost total break between Trotsky and Martov – whom, by the way, Trotsky always respected as a political intellect – and at the same time a break between all of us left Internationalists and the Martov group.

At this period there came to be so many political points of contact between Trotsky and myself that we were, I think, at our closest; it fell to me to represent his viewpoint in all discussions with the other editors and theirs with him. He and I very often spoke on the same platform at various *émigré* student gatherings, we jointly edited Party proclamations; in short we were in very close alliance.

I have always regarded Trotsky as a great man. Who, indeed, can doubt it? In Paris he had grown greatly in stature in my eyes as a statesman and in the future he grew even more. I do not know whether it was because I knew him better and he was better able to demonstrate the full measure of his powers when working on a grander scale or because in fact the experience of the revolution and its problems really did mature him and enlarge the sweep of his wings.

The agitational work of spring 1917 does not fall within the scope of these memoirs but I should say that under the influence of his tremendous activity and blinding success certain people close to Trotsky were even inclined to see in him the real leader of the Russian revolution. Thus for instance the late M. S. Uritsky,[16] whose attitude to Trotsky was one of great respect, once said to me and I think to Manuilsky:[17] 'Now that the great revolution has come one feels that however intelligent Lenin may be he begins to fade beside the genius of Trotsky.' This estimation seemed to me incorrect, not because it exaggerated Trotsky's gifts and his force of character but because the extent of Lenin's political genius was then still not obvious. Yet it is true that during that period, after the thunderous success of his arrival in Russia and before the July days, Lenin did keep rather in the background, not speaking often, not writing much, but largely engaged in directing organizational work in the Bolshevik camp, whilst Trotsky thundered forth at meetings in Petrograd.

Trotsky's most obvious gifts were his talents as an orator and as a writer. I regard Trotsky as probably the greatest orator of our age. In my time I have heard all the greatest parliamentarians and popular tribunes of socialism and very many famous orators of the bourgeois world and I would find it difficult to name any of them, except Jaurès[18] (Bebel[19] I only heard when he was an old man), whom I could put in the same class as Trotsky.

His impressive appearance, his handsome, sweeping gestures, the powerful rhythm of his speech, his loud but never fatiguing voice, the remarkable coherence and literary skill of his phrasing, the richness of imagery, scalding irony, his soaring pathos, his rigid logic, clear as polished steel – those are Trotsky's virtues as a speaker. He can speak in lapidary phrases, or throw off a few unusually well-aimed shafts and he can give a magnificent set-piece political speech of the kind that previously I had only heard from Jaurès. I have seen Trotsky speaking for two and a half to three hours in front of a totally silent, standing audience listening as though spellbound to his monumental political treatise. Most of what Trotsky had to say I knew already and naturally every politician often has to repeat the same ideas again and again in front of new crowds, yet every time Trotsky managed to clothe the same thought in a different form. I do not know whether Trotsky made so many speeches when he became War Minister of our great republic during the revolution and civil war: it is most probable that his organizational work and tireless journeying from end to end of the vast front left him little time for oratory, but even then Trotsky was above all a great political agitator. His articles and books are, as it were, frozen speech – he was literary in his oratory and an orator in literature.

It is thus obvious why Trotsky was also an outstanding publicist, although of course it frequently happened that the spell-binding quality of his actual speech was somewhat lost in his writing.

As regards his inner qualities as a leader Trotsky, as I have said, was clumsy and ill-suited to the small-scale work of Party organization. This defect was to be glaringly evident in the future, since it was above all the work in the illegal underground of such men as Lenin, Chernov[20] and Martov which later enabled their parties to contend for hegemony in Russia and later, perhaps, all over the world. Trotsky was hampered by the very definite limitations of his own personality.

Trotsky as a man is prickly and overbearing. However, after Trotsky's merger with the Bolsheviks, it was only in his attitude to Lenin that Trotsky always showed – and continues to show – a tactful pliancy which is touching. With the modesty of all truly great men he acknowledges Lenin's primacy.

On the other hand as a man of political counsel Trotsky's gifts are equal to his rhetorical powers. It could hardly be otherwise, since however skilful an orator may be, if his speech is not illuminated by thought he is no more than a sterile virtuoso and all his oratory is as a tinkling cymbal. It may not be quite so necessary for an orator to be inspired by love, as the apostle Paul maintains, for he may be filled with hate, but it is essential for him to be a *thinker*. Only a great politician can be a great orator, and since Trotsky is chiefly a political orator, his speeches are naturally the expression of political thinking.

It seems to me that Trotsky is incomparably more orthodox than Lenin, although many people may find this strange. Trotsky's political career has been somewhat tortuous: he was neither a Menshevik nor a Bolshevik but sought the middle way before merging his brook in the Bolshevik river, and yet in fact Trotsky has always been guided by the precise rules of revolutionary Marxism. Lenin is both masterful and creative in the realm of political thought and has very often formulated entirely new lines of policy which subsequently proved highly effective in achieving results. Trotsky is not remarkable for such boldness of thought: he takes revolutionary

Marxism and draws from it the conclusions applicable to a given situation. He is as bold as can be in opposing liberalism and semi-socialism, but he is no innovator.

At the same time Lenin is much more of an opportunist, in the profoundest sense of the word. This may again sound odd – was not Trotsky once associated with the Mensheviks, those notorious opportunists? But the Mensheviks' opportunism was simply the political flabbiness of a petty-bourgeois party. I am not referring to this sort of opportunism; I am referring to that sense of reality which leads one now and then to alter one's tactics, to that tremendous sensitivity to the demands of the time which prompts Lenin at one moment to sharpen both edges of his sword, at another to place it in its sheath.

Trotsky has less of this ability; his path to revolution has followed a straight line. These differing characteristics showed up in the famous clash between the two leaders of the great Russian revolution over the peace of Brest-Litovsk.[21]

It is usual to say of Trotsky that he is ambitious. This, of course, is utter nonsense. I remember Trotsky making a very significant remark in connection with Chernov's acceptance of a ministerial portfolio: 'What despicable ambition – to abandon one's place in history in exchange for the untimely offer of a ministerial post.' In that, I think, lay all of Trotsky. There is not a drop of vanity in him, he is totally indifferent to any title or to the trappings of power; he is, however, boundlessly jealous of his own role in history and in that sense he is ambitious. Here he is I think as sincere as he is in his natural love of power.

Lenin is not in the least ambitious either. I do not believe that Lenin ever steps back and looks at himself, never even thinks what posterity will say about him – he simply gets on with his job. He does it through the exercise of power, not because he finds power sweet but because he is convinced of the rightness of what he is doing and cannot bear that anyone should harm his cause. His ambitiousness stems from his colossal certainty of the rectitude of his principles and too, perhaps, from an inability (a very useful trait in a politician) to see things from his opponent's point of view. Lenin never regards an argument as a mere discussion; for him an argument is always a clash between different classes or different groups, as it were a clash between different species of humanity. An argument for him is always a struggle, which under certain circumstances may develop into a fight. Lenin always welcomes the transition from a struggle to a fight.

In contrast to Lenin, Trotsky is undoubtedly often prone to step back and watch himself. Trotsky treasures his historical role and would probably be ready to make any personal sacrifice, not excluding the greatest sacrifice of all – that of his life – in order to go down in human memory surrounded by the aureole of a genuine revolutionary leader. His ambition has the same characteristic as that of Lenin, with the difference that he is more often liable to make mistakes, lacking as he does Lenin's almost infallible instinct, and being a man of choleric temperament he is liable, although only temporarily, to be blinded by passion, whilst Lenin, always on an even keel and always in command of himself, is virtually incapable of being distracted by irritation.

It would be wrong to imagine, however, that the second great leader of the Russian revolution is inferior to his colleague in everything: there are, for instance, aspects in which Trotsky incontestably surpasses him – he is more brilliant, he is clearer, he is more active. Lenin is fitted as no one else to take the chair at the Council of Peoples' Commissars and to guide the world revolution with the touch of genius, but he could never have coped with the titanic mission[22] which Trotsky took upon his own shoulders, with those lightning moves from place to place, those astounding speeches, those fanfares of on-the-spot orders, that role of being the unceasing electrifier of a weakening army, now at one spot, now at another. There is not a man on earth who could have replaced Trotsky in that respect.

Whenever a truly great revolution occurs, a great people will always find the right actor to play every part and one of the signs of greatness in our revolution is the fact that the Communist Party has produced from its own ranks or has borrowed from other parties and incorporated into its own organism sufficient outstanding personalities who were suited as no others to fulfil whatever political function was called for.

And two of the strongest of the strong, totally identified with their roles, are Lenin and Trotsky.

NOTES

So much heat and polemic still surround the name of Lev Bronstein, alias Trotsky, that it is impossible in such a small compass to do more than try to indicate Trotsky's position and standing in Russia at the moment when Lunacharsky wrote this profile in late 1918. This point in time was perhaps the zenith of Trotsky's extraordinary career. His progress until then had been a classic example of what can be achieved in politics through a combination of ambition, outstanding intelligence and sheer cheek. Although he had sided with the Mensheviks at the 1903 Party split, Trotsky was incapable of being tagged with a factional label for long and in the pre-1917 squabbles he was always something of a one-man splinter group aligned somewhere in the centre between Mensheviks and Bolsheviks.

But as Lunacharsky says, Trotsky's heart was never in the arid wrangling of *émigré* politics, enlivened only by a spell of intoxicating action in the 1905 revolution. With his compulsive urge for the limelight Trotsky needed to be in the centre of the stage mastering a packed house, or in the thick of action where the fray was hottest. Both these chances were given to him in 1917. Lenin had not much time for the Petrograd Soviet as a political force in that revolutionary year; it was left to Trotsky to demonstrate his amazing ability to both stimulate and control this large, politically uneducated and somewhat unstable assembly and to give it sufficient political credibility to become, after the fiasco of the one-day life of the Constituent Assembly, the sovereign body of all Russia. When in October the need came for action, Trotsky's role as leader of the Military Revolutionary Committee made of him the man who, under Lenin's direction, physically executed the Bolshevik seizure of power: for a few days Trotsky virtually *was* the Russian Revolution.

By contrast his first job as Commissar for Foreign Affairs, the Brest-Litovsk peace negotiations, was something of a disaster. Torn between revolutionary internationalism and the agonizing prospect of ceding vast areas of Russian territory to Germany and Austria, Trotsky tried to evade the issue by his 'Neither peace nor war' thesis, in the hope that the Germans would somehow stop their advance into Russia. The move failed and the Germans pressed on. Faced with the threat of Lenin's resignation if the peace treaty were not signed, Trotsky stood down with bad grace and the humiliating German terms were accepted. Smarting under his failure as a diplomat, Trotsky the Marxist internationalist then threw his enormous energy and thirst for action into the job of being the military chief of the new Russian State. As first Commissar for War and the virtual creator of the Red Army out of a demoralized rabble and a hostile officer corps Trotsky was a brilliant success. Organizing, improvising, exhorting, Trotsky raced tirelessly from end to end of his vast country in an armoured train. One of the greatest amateur generals of all time, Trotsky beat the professionals – the 'White' Russian generals and the well-armed Allied intervention forces – at their own game. It was at the height of the Civil War that Lunacharsky wrote his profile of Trotsky, at the pinnacle of Trotsky's success. And there it is kindest to leave the man whom the American John Reed in a transport of enthusiasm called 'the greatest Jew since Christ,' and who in 1940 died in exile in Mexico, from a blow with an ice-axe dealt by an emissary of Stalin.

1. THE EVENTS OF JANUARY: Refers to 'Bloody Sunday' (9 January 1905) when a peaceful workers' procession, headed by the priest Father Gapon, marched through Petersburg to present a petition to the Tsar and was shot down by troops.

2. PARVUS: Dr Alexander L. Helphand, alias Parvus (1867–1924). Of Russo-German origin, simultaneously a brilliant revolutionary schemer and a businessman, Parvus was the go-between who channelled German government funds to the Bolsheviks with the aim of disrupting Russia's war effort.

3. SMALL AND CHEAP NEWSPAPER: This newspaper, called

Nachalo (*The Beginning*) replaced *Iskra* (*The Spark*) as the party journal. It began publication on 10 November 1905 in St Petersburg. Besides Trotsky and Parvus, Dan and Martov also contributed to it.

4. THE STOCKHOLM CONGRESS: The 4th Congress of the Russian Social Democratic party, held in April 1906. Called the 'Unification' Congress, as it temporarily healed the breach between the Bolsheviks and the Mensheviks and re-admitted the 'Bund' (q.v. below) to the party.

5. QUASI-KADET TENDENCIES: '*Kadet*', from the Russian initial letters of the words 'Constitutional Democrats', was the name of the left-wing liberal political party founded in 1905. The party dominated the first Duma in 1906 and in subsequent Dumas formed the chief opposition party. The party, particularly its leader Milyukov played a major part in the Provisional Government. The Kadets were outlawed by the Bolsheviks at their seizure of power in October–November 1917.

6. LIQUIDATORS: Lenin's term of opprobrium for those right-wing Mensheviks who after 1905 wanted the Party to give up its illegal political activities and concentrate on legal means of advancing the workers' cause, i.e. in trades unions, cooperatives etc.

7. SEMKOVSKY: Semyon Yulievich Bronstein, alias Semkovsky (1882–?). Journalist. A Menshevik until 1920, then joined the Bolshevik party.

8. SKOBELIEV: Matvey Ivanovich Skobeliev (1885–1939). Joined the Social Democratic party in 1903, worked as an agitator in Baku. Menshevik deputy to the Fourth Duma, 1912. Minister of Labour in the Provisional Government. Emigrated in 1920. Returned to U.S.S.R. 1922. Liquidated in the thirties purge.

9. COPENHAGEN CONGRESS: Congress of the Second International, 1910.

10. VORWÄRTS: (*Forward*) Central organ of the German Social Democratic party (S.P.D.).

11. RYAZANOV: David Borisovich Goldendach, alias Ryazanov (1870–1938). An early, non-factional Social Democrat. On the war issue was an internationalist. Joined Trotsky's 'Interdistrict' group (q.v. below) that stood outside the Bolshevik–Menshevik factional struggle. Member of the Bolshevik party, 1917. Later Director of the Marx–Engels–Lenin Institute. Expelled from the Party and exiled in 1931.

12. OUR WORD: ('*Nashe Slovo*') Non-factional, though largely Menshevik, Russian Social Democratic newspaper founded in Paris in 1914. Under various names it was published until 1917.

13. DEFEATISTS: Those who supported Lenin's attitude to the outcome of the First World War, i.e. that the revolution would be best served if Russia were beaten, thus hastening the political and social dissolution of the old regime.

14. INTERNATIONALISTS: A minority of socialists throughout Europe who urged the working class – without the least effect – not to support the war between the 'capitalist' governments of their countries.

15. DEFENCISTS: The largely Menshevik grouping, headed by Plekhanov, which adopted a patriotic attitude to Russia's war effort against Germany. In their view victory for imperialist Germany would mean the extinction of Socialism in all European countries, including Russia.

16. URITSKY: Moisei Solomonovich Uritsky (1873–1918). See below pp. 123–9.

17. MANUILSKY: Dmitri Zakharevich Manuilsky (1883–1959). Became a Social Democrat 1903. Belonged (with Lunacharsky) to the left-wing 'Forward' group and the 'Interdistrict' group. Joined the Bolsheviks 1917. Central Committee of the Ukrainian C.P. since 1920. Ukrainian delegate to the U.N. and 'foreign minister' of the Ukraine 1944–52.

18. EXCEPT JAURÈS: Jean Auguste Jaurès (1899–1914). Professor of philosophy, Toulouse University. French Socialist Party leader. Founder and first editor of *L'Humanité*. Assassinated at the outbreak of the First World War for his anti-militarist views.

19. BEBEL: August Bebel (1830–1913). Early German socialist. Chairman of the S.P.D. Prominent in the Second International.

20. CHERNOV: Viktor Mikhailovich Chernov (1873–1952). Radical thinker and leader of the Socialist Revolutionary (S.R.) party, established in 1902. Minister of Agriculture in Provisional Government. After the split-off of the Left S.Rs, who supported the Bolshevik seizure of power in 1917, Chernov's Right S.R. party won a majority in the Constituent Assembly. Fled Russia during the Civil War. Died in New York.

21. CLASH . . . OVER THE PEACE OF BREST-LITOVSK:

Lenin, aware of the total collapse of the Russian army in 1918 and of the consequences of a German seizure of Petrograd, demanded peace at any price; Trotsky, chief Bolshevik negotiator with the Germans at Brest-Litovsk, refused to sign the Treaty and proclaimed a state of 'neither peace nor war', i.e. a unilateral armistice declared by Russia and withdrawal of Russian troops. Lenin won, after furious debate in the Party Central Committee, and Sokolnikov and Chicherin signed the harsh peace terms on behalf of Russia.

22. TITANIC MISSION: Refers to Trotsky's appointment as Commissar for War (1918–1922), when he virtually created the Red Army and beat the combined Allied and 'White' Russian forces.

GRIGORII OVSEYEVICH ZINOVIEV

When I arrived in Geneva in 1904 I joined the editorial staff of the central organ of the Bolshevik section of the Party. At that time we were busily engaged in seeking agents and in organizing cells among as many of the *émigré* student colonies as possible. It became apparent that this was not the easiest of tasks, as the Mensheviks were strongly entrenched everywhere. Furthermore the numerous Bundists[1] and the socialist groups of other non-Russian nationalities were hand-in-glove with the Mensheviks. No one supported us; we were the most isolated and the least accommodating of all the parties. Consequently we cherished every ally we could find. From Berne we received an enthusiastic letter with an offer of service, signed by 'Kazakov and Radomyslsky'.

When I went to Berne to give a lecture, I naturally made it my first task to meet these Bernese Bolsheviks. At the time Kazakov appeared to be the keener of the two. Subsequently he played a certain part in the history of our Party under the surname of Svyagin. He worked in Kronstadt, was exiled and, I think, sentenced to hard labour. While in detention during the war he joined the French army and was killed.

Radomyslsky, on the other hand, did not immediately strike me as very promising. He was rather a fat young man, pale and sickly, who suffered from shortness of breath and was, I thought, too phlegmatic in temperament. The loquacious Kazakov never allowed him to get a word in edgeways. However, after we had been in permanent touch with them for some time we became convinced that Radomyslsky was an efficient lad and we came to treat Kazakov as what he was – a very glib talker.

When I arrived in Petersburg after the revolution I learned that Radomyslsky, under the name of Grigorii, was working in the Vassilevsky Island District and working very well, that he was a candidate for the Petersburg committee, which he entered, if I am not mistaken, very soon after my arrival. I was very pleased to hear such good reports of our young student from Switzerland. I soon met him personally and at his request I edited a whole series of his translations.

In the midst of some great dispute during the stormy election campaign for the Stockholm 'Unification' Congress, Zinoviev and I spoke up jointly in defence of our line. It was here that I first heard him addressing a meeting. I immediately appreciated his ability and was also somewhat surprised: usually so quiet and rather delicate, he warmed during his speech and spoke with great animation. He had a massive and unusually resonant tenor voice. Even then I realized that this voice could dominate an audience of thousands. To these remarkable physical qualities was plainly added an ease and fluency of speech which sprang from mental resourcefulness and a remarkable grasp of logic, from the ability to see his speech as a whole and not to allow details to dull his grip on the main theme. In time comrade Zinoviev systematically developed all these qualities and made himself into the outstanding master of the spoken word that we know today.

Naturally Zinoviev's speeches are not as rich or as full of new ideas as the real leader of the revolution, Lenin, and he cannot compete in graphic power with Trotsky, but with the exception of these two orators, Zinoviev has no equals. I do not know of a single S.R. or Menshevik who is in the same class as Zinoviev (again, except Trotsky) as a crowd orator, an orator of the streets or of the mass meeting.

As a journalist Zinoviev is marked by the same qualities as Zinoviev the orator, namely the clarity and accessibility of his thought and a smooth and easy style, although what makes Zinoviev so particularly valuable as a tribune – the remarkable, tireless, dominating power of his voice – is lost in print.

I do not believe, however, that Zinoviev owes the high place which he already occupied in our Party long before the revolution and the historic part that he is playing now merely, or even chiefly, to his talents as a speaker and journalist. At a very early stage Lenin came to rely on him not only as a politically experienced friend who was wholly inspired with Vladimir Ilyich's own spirit, but as a man who had a profound understanding of the fundamentals of Bolshevism and who possessed a political intellect of the highest order. Zinoviev is undoubtedly one of the principal counsellors of our Central Committee and belongs unquestionably to the four or five men who constitute the political brain of the Party.

As a person Zinoviev is an extremely humane man, a good man who is highly intelligent, but he is literally rather ashamed of these qualities of his and is sometimes over-ready to buckle on the armour of revolutionary hardness.

Zinoviev has always acted as Lenin's faithful henchman and has followed him everywhere. The Mensheviks have affected a slightly scornful attitude to Zinoviev for being just such a dedicated henchman. Perhaps we Forwardists were also slightly infected by this attitude. We knew that Zinoviev was an excellent Party worker, but we knew little of him as a political thinker and we too often used to say of him that he followed Lenin as the thread follows a needle.

The first time that I heard a completely different assessment of Zinoviev was from Ryazanov. I met Ryazanov in Zürich, where Zinoviev was also living, and fell into conversation with him about various leading Party members. Ryazanov mentioned that he often met Zinoviev: 'He is a tremendous worker. He works hard and intelligently and by now he is so well versed in economics and sociology that he has far surpassed most of the Mensheviks in those subjects, even, I would say, all the Mensheviks.' This commendation from such a scholar as Ryazanov, incontestably the most learned man in the Party, was once again a pleasant and unexpected surprise to me.

When I finally joined the main stream of Bolshevism, it was to Zinoviev in Zürich that I turned. We recalled our earlier good relations and agreed on the terms of a political alliance in literally half an hour.

The above short chapter from Volume I of *The Great Revolution* is so far from being exhaustive, even as a 'profile', that I think I should add a few more lines at this point.

Many Bolsheviks, perhaps indeed all of them, have grown enormously in stature since the revolution: great tasks, great responsibilities and broad perspectives break only the weaker vessels and always serve to enlarge people who have any degree of intelligence and energy.

Yet possibly not one of our Party figures has gained so much in stature during the revolution as Grigorii Ovseyevich Zinoviev.

Lenin and Trotsky have, of course, become the most widely known (whether they are loved or hated) personalities of our epoch, almost all over the globe. Zinoviev recedes slightly in comparison with them, but on the other hand Lenin and Trotsky have so long been regarded in our ranks as men of such enormous talent, as such incontestable leaders, that their colossal increase in stature during the revolution can hardly have evoked any particular surprise. Zinoviev, too, was greatly respected. Everybody regarded him as Lenin's closest assistant and confidant. Knowing him to be a talented speaker and journalist, as a man who was hard-working, quick-witted, wholly devoted to the social revolution and to his Party, anybody could have predicted that Zinoviev would play a major role in the revolution and in a revolutionary government. But Zinoviev has undoubtedly surpassed many people's expectations.

I well remember how during the organization of the Third International the Menshevik Dan, then still in Russia, said with wry sarcasm: 'What a magnificent advertisement for the Third International – to be headed by Zinoviev.' Of course the First International had been headed by Marx and there can be no comparison between them, but it would be interesting to know whom the scornful Dan was thinking of as the head of the Second International? The Second International had at various times some very big men in charge of it but the chairman of the Third International has no grounds to fear comparison with any of them. Here his enormous abilities have been given full play and here he has acquired his unquestionable authority.

From the very beginning it was obvious that Zinoviev was not discouraged by the crushing responsibility of the post with which he had been entrusted. From the start, and in increasing measure with time, he has displayed astounding level-headedness in the discharge of his functions. Always steady, ever ingenious, he has emerged with honour from the most trying circumstances. People often say with a smile of Zinoviev that he is a man who has acquired such vast experience as a parliamentarian that he can easily dominate any opposition. Zinoviev's skill as a chairman has indeed earned general admiration, but of course the occasionally fairly difficult problems of diplomacy which Zinoviev has to solve are eased for him to a significant degree by the fact that in the ranks of the Third International there rarely arise problems which cannot be dealt with within the framework of Party discipline and links of profound friendship.

There is not a single element in the whole vast current of affairs of the International which escapes Zinoviev's attention. In so far as one person is capable of grasping world politics, he is that person. Who does not know Zinoviev's revolutionary determination in all international controversies, his implacability, his exacting demands, his strict adherence to principle, thanks to which many of our foreign neighbours – and at times renegades within our own ranks – talk of the iron hand of Moscow, of dictatorial Russian methods? Yet whilst being firm where necessary, Zinoviev simultaneously displays the maximum of adaptability and ability to compromise in rebuilding a shattered world.

To this one must add that Zinoviev has won the reputation of being one of the most remarkable orators on the international scene – a very difficult feat. It is one thing to speak in one's native tongue, as do the overwhelming majority of our comrades in the Comintern, but quite another to hold forth in a foreign language. Although he has a good grasp of German, Zinoviev still, as he himself stresses, cannot speak it like a German. It is all the more astonishing, and all the more to his credit, therefore, that his speeches always make a colossal impression not only by their content but by the force and precision of their delivery. Not for nothing did the bourgeois Press state after Zinoviev's famous three-hour speech, made in the very heart of Germany at the *Parteitag* in Halle: 'This man possesses a demonic power of eloquence.'

Zinoviev also brings these qualities of firmness, tactical skill and calmness to the very difficult task of running the administration of Petrograd, which has made him irreplaceable in this job, too, despite the Comintern's frequent requests to the Central Committee that Zinoviev should work full-time for them.

I should like to mention one more characteristic of Zinoviev – his positively romantic dedication to his Party. The normally sober and businesslike Zinoviev rises to dithyrambic heights of love for the Party in his solemn speeches made on the occasion of various Party anniversaries.

There is no doubt whatever that in Zinoviev the Russian workers' movement has put forth not only one of its own great leaders but has also, alongside Lenin and Trotsky, produced one of the decisive figures of the world-wide workers' movement.

NOTES

Because of the scandalous forgery attached to his name by *émigré* Russian plotters, Zinoviev (1883–1936) is better known outside Russia than many other more interesting and sympathetic figures in the Russian revolutionary movement. As Lunacharsky says, until 1917 Zinoviev was known even to his fellow-Bolsheviks as little more than Lenin's shadow. He was the leader's inseparable amanuensis and *aide-de-camp* who literally accompanied him everywhere, a role he had taken up in Switzerland during the second emigration after the 1905 revolution. He travelled with Lenin to Russia in the famous 'sealed train' in April 1917 and was the only person to go with Lenin when they were forced into hiding as a result of the abortive armed insurrection during the 'July Days'. Having fled Petrograd, he and Lenin shared a tent beside a pond near the border with Finland, pretending to be two Finnish farm-hands. When it came to real action, however, Zinoviev shrank from the proposed revolutionary *coup* and on 10 October 1917 he and Kamenev were the only two Central Committee members to vote against Lenin on the issue of staging the armed move which was to place the Bolsheviks in power.

Zinoviev took virtually no part in the actual October revolution and Lenin did not forget his faint-heartedness: when the Council of Peoples' Commissars (Lenin's cabinet) was formed, there was no portfolio for Zinoviev. However, he was elected chairman of the Executive Committee of the Petrograd Soviet in 1919, which made him the boss of the great city. In the relative safety of this office Zinoviev, who had shrunk from the thought of exposure in the firing-line in 1917, was ruthless in harrying the 'enemies of the people'. He remained at the job until 1926, when Stalin saw to it that he was removed. His other main post for the same period was as chairman of the Third International or Comintern, the body devoted to fostering revolution abroad. (It was because of Zinoviev's tenure of this job that his name was attached to the notorious 'letter'.)

A born schemer, Zinoviev first sided with Stalin and Kamenev against Trotsky in the struggle for succession that followed Lenin's death, but he then made a serious miscalculation by thinking that by switching allegiance to Trotsky he could unseat Stalin. Stalin combined with Bukharin to topple Zinoviev, who was deprived of all his offices and expelled from the Party. He climbed back in again, only to be expelled again and once more re-admitted. Stalin finally dealt with Zinoviev by imprisoning him in 1935 for 'moral complicity' in the murder of Kirov and then made sure that he would not survive by arraigning him at the first 'purge' trial in 1936, at which Zinoviev was condemned and shot.

1. BUNDISTS: Members of the '*Bund*', the abbreviated name (it means 'league' or 'union' in Yiddish and German) of the socialist General Jewish Workers' Union, founded at Vilna in 1897. The *Bund* took part in the 1903 2nd Congress of Russian Social Democratic Party, but walked out when it failed to be recognized as sole representative of Jewish workers in Russia. Re-affiliated to Party in 1906, the *Bund* supported the Mensheviks. Led by Liber and others it played a big part in 1905 and 1917 revolutions. In 1920 the majority of Bundists joined the Bolshevik Party; the non-Bolshevik minority was politically suppressed.

GEORGII VALENTINOVICH PLEKHANOV

Some encounters with Georgii Valentinovich Plekhanov

I have few personal recollections of Georgii Valentinovich. Our meetings were infrequent, although they were not devoid of significance and I gladly record my memories of him.

In 1893 I left Russia for Zürich, as I felt that I could only acquire the education I needed by going abroad. My friends the Lindfors gave me a letter of introduction to Pavel Alexandrovich Axelrod.

Axelrod and his family received me with delightful hospitality. By then I was a more or less convinced Marxist and considered myself a member of the Social Democratic party (I was eighteen and had begun work as an agitator and propagandist two years before going abroad). I am very much indebted to Axelrod for my education in socialism and, however far apart he and I may have moved subsequently, I look upon him with gratitude as one of my most influential teachers. Axelrod was full of awe and reverence for Plekhanov and spoke of him with adoration. This, added to the impression of brilliance that I had already gained from reading *Our Differences*[1] and various other articles by Plekhanov, filled me with an uneasy, disturbing sense of expectation at the prospect of meeting this great man.

At last Plekhanov came from Geneva to Zürich, brought there by a dispute among the Polish socialists on the nationality question. The nationally-minded socialists in Zürich were headed by Jodko.[2] Our future comrades were led by Rosa Luxemburg,[3] then a brilliant student at Zürich University. Plekhanov was to pronounce on the conflict. For some reason his train was late, so that my first sight of Plekhanov was destined to be slightly theatrical. The meeting had already begun; with rather wearisome emphasis Jodko had been defending his viewpoint for half an hour when into the Eintracht Hall strode Plekhanov.

That was twenty-eight years ago. Plekhanov must have been slightly over thirty. He was a well-proportioned rather slim man in an impeccable frock coat, with a handsome face made particularly striking by his brilliant eyes and – his most marked feature – by thick, shaggy eyebrows. Later at the Stuttgart Congress one newspaper spoke of Plekhanov as '*eine aristokratische Erscheinung*'. Indeed in Plekhanov's appearance, in his diction, his tone of voice and his whole bearing there was the ineradicable stamp of the gentry – he was a gentleman from head to toe. This was apt to offend some people's proletarian instincts, but when one remembered that this gentleman was an extreme revolutionary and one of the pioneers of the workers' movement, Plekhanov's aristocratic air became something impressive and moving: 'Look what sort of people are on our side.'

I have no intention of writing a character-study of Plekhanov – that is a task for another occasion – but I would note in passing that in Plekhanov's very appearance and manner something made me, a young man, involuntarily think: Herzen[4] must have been like that.

Plekhanov sat down at Axelrod's table, where I was also sitting, but we exchanged no more than a few sentences.

Plekhanov's speech itself rather disappointed me, perhaps by contrast with Rosa's speech which was as sharp as a razor-blade and as brilliant as silver. When the loud applause for her speech had died down, old Greulich,[5] even then grey-haired, even then looking like Abraham (I saw him, by the way, twenty-five years later looking almost as lively as he had on that occasion although, alas, by then neither he nor Plekhanov were progressive socialists) mounted the rostrum and said in a specially solemn tone: 'Now comrade Plekhanov will speak. He will speak in French. His speech will be translated but, my friends, please try and maintain absolute silence and follow his speech with attention.'

This appeal by the chairman for reverential silence and

the huge ovation with which Georgii Valentinovich was greeted combined to move me to tears. A mere youth, which made it pardonable, I was extremely proud of my great fellow-countryman. But his speech, I repeat, rather disappointed me.

For political reasons Plekhanov wanted to adopt a mid-way position. As a Russian he obviously found it awkward to speak out against the Polish national spirit, although he was theoretically wholly on Rosa Luxemburg's side. At all events he emerged from this difficult situation with honour and with great skill, playing the part of the wise conciliator.

Georgii Valentinovich then stayed for several more days in Zürich and at the risk of seeming rude I lingered whole days at the Axelrods' to seize every possible chance of talking to him.

The opportunities were numerous. Plekhanov loved talking. I was a boy who was well-read, not unintelligent and extremely eager. In spite of my awe of Plekhanov I got on my high horse and, as it were, invited combat on various philosophical questions. Plekhanov liked this; sometimes he would deal playfully with me like a big dog with a puppy and would knock me on my back with an unexpected swipe of his great paw, sometimes he grew angry and sometimes he would expound his views with great earnestness.

Plekhanov was an absolutely incomparable conversationalist in the brilliance of his wit, the wealth of his knowledge, the ease with which he could mobilize the most enormous concentration of mental power on any subject. The Germans have a word '*geistreich*' – rich of mind. It exactly describes Plekhanov.

I should mention that Plekhanov did not shake my faith in the great significance of 'left realism', i.e. Avenarius's[6] philosophy. He said jokingly to me: 'Let's talk about Kant instead, if you really want to flounder about in the theory of knowledge – he at least was a man.' Although Plekhanov was capable of dealing an intellectual knock-out blow on occasions, he was also prone to strike off-target.

However, these talks had an immeasurably great influence on me when Plekhanov dwelt on the great Idealist philosophers Fichte,[7] Schelling[8] and Hegel.[9]

Naturally I was already well aware of the enormous significance of Hegel in the history of socialism and of the impossibility of having a proper grasp of the Marxist philosophy of history without a sound acquaintance with Hegel.

Later Plekhanov was to accuse me in one of our public disputes of not having studied Hegel properly. Partly thanks to Plekhanov I had in fact read Hegel with some thoroughness, but I would have done so in any case, as befitted an aspiring socialist theoretician. Fichte and Schelling were another matter. I thought it quite adequate to have read about them in histories of philosophy, considering them to be a dead letter and not worth studying. Plekhanov, however, spoke of them with unexpected enthusiasm. Without for a moment relapsing into any heresy such as 'Back to Fichte!' (later proclaimed by Struve), he nevertheless held forth to me in such a fervent, glorious paean to Fichte and Schelling as the architects of a monumental philosophical edifice that I immediately ran to the Zürich national library and plunged into reading the works of those great Idealists, who were to leave such a stamp not only on my whole philosophical outlook but indeed on my entire personality.

It is a great shame that Plekhanov did no more than touch on the Idealist philosophers. He knew them exhaustively, indeed with astonishing exactitude, and could have written a book on them which would certainly have been no less brilliant than his book on the materialist precursors of Marxism. It is true, I think, that in Plekhanov's undoubtedly rather Bazarov-like mind, of the forerunners of Marxism his favourites d'Holbach[10] and Helvétius[11] were dearer to him than the Idealists. But anyone who imagined that he ignored that other great root of Marxism would be doing Plekhanov an injustice.

Georgii Valentinovich suggested that I should visit him to continue our talks; but it was a year or so before I was able to go to Geneva from Paris. Those, too, were happy days. Georgii Valentinovich was then writing his foreword to the *Communist Manifesto* and had become very interested in art. I had always been passionately interested in it and consequently the chief theme of our talks was the dependence of the cultural superstructure on the economic base of society, especially where art was concerned. I used to meet him in his study in the rue de Candole and sometimes in the Café Landolt where we would spend hours over many a mug of beer.

I remember one incident which made a tremendous impression on me. Plekhanov was pacing up and down his study explaining something. Suddenly he walked over to a cupboard, took out a large album, laid it on the table in front of me and opened it. It contained some wonderful engravings by Boucher, extremely frivolous and – by my standards of those days – almost pornographic; I at once said something to that effect, that here was a typical indication of the decadence of a ruling class on the eve of revolution.

'Yes,' said Plekhanov, looking at me with his glittering eyes, 'but look how superb they are – what style, what life, what elegance, what sensuality.'

I shall not attempt to record the rest of the conversation – it would mean writing a minor treatise on rococo art. I can only say that Plekhanov more or less anticipated all of Hausenstein's main conclusions, although I do not recall him telling me exactly whether or not Boucher's art was fundamentally a bourgeois art that had been merely transplanted into a framework of court life.

To me his aesthetic perception was astounding – his powers of judgement on matters of art were wide-ranging and unprejudiced. Plekhanov's taste was, I think, infallible. On any work of art that he disliked he could express himself in two words, with an absolutely lethal irony which totally disarmed you if you happened to disagree with him. About works of art which pleased him Plekhanov spoke with such precision, at times with such excitement that it became obvious why he was an influential writer on the history of art. His relatively modest studies, dealing only with a few periods, have become one of the cornerstones of subsequent work in that field.

From no book, from no museum, have I ever gained so much stimulation and insight as from those talks of mine with Georgii Valentinovich.

Unfortunately our subsequent meetings took place in rather less happy circumstances, where we encountered each other as political enemies.

I did not meet Plekhanov again until the Stuttgart Congress. The Bolshevik delegation had appointed me their official representative on the very important committee set up to work out the Party's policy towards the trades unions. Plekhanov represented the Mensheviks. At the very start a dispute arose within the Russian delegation. The majority voted for our viewpoint and the waverers eventually swung over to our side. The matter was in no sense a personal victory of mine over Plekhanov: he defended his thesis brilliantly, but the thesis itself was unacceptable. Plekhanov insisted that close alliance between the Party and the trades unions might be detrimental to the Party, that the task of the trades unions was to improve the workers' lot within the capitalist system whereas the Party's task was to destroy that system itself. He advocated independence. The opposing tendency was headed by the Belgian De Brouckère.[12] (De Brouckère was then a very left-wing socialist whose thinking had much in common with ours, although he was later to deviate.) De Brouckère stood for the need to penetrate the trade-union movement with a socialist consciousness of the indissoluble unity of the working class, the guiding role of the Party and so on. In the reigning atmosphere of heated discussion of the general strike as a fighting weapon, everyone was tending to reconsider their previous views. We were all aware that parliamentarism was becoming a more and more inadequate weapon, that without the trades unions the Party would never accomplish the revolution and that after the revolution the trades unions were bound to play a major part in rebuilding a new world. As a result, Plekhanov's attitude, represented at the international level by Guesde,[13] was ultimately rejected both by our committee and by the Congress itself.

To my surprise I detected a certain trace of the 'Old

Believer' in Plekhanov's political attitudes. For the first time his orthodoxy seemed slightly ossified and it occurred to me that politics were far from being Plekhanov's strong suit. One might have deduced this in any case from the way in which he wavered between one and the other of the Party's two main factions.

We next met at the Stockholm Congress, where this characteristic behaviour of Plekhanov's became all too evident. He was far from being a convinced Menshevik at this congress. In part his aim was conciliationist. He stood for Party unity (this was, after all, the 'Unification' congress) and maintained that if revolutionary feeling were to increase in Russia the Mensheviks would find no allies except from the ranks of the Bolsheviks. On the other hand he was frightened by the rigidity of the Bolsheviks' position. In his opinion Bolshevism was not orthodox. Indeed the main feature which differentiated the two factions at that time was their policy on the peasantry.

The scheme of the revolution as the Mensheviks envisaged it was as follows: a bourgeois revolution was in progress in Russia, which would culminate in a constitutional monarchy, or at best in a bourgeois republic. The working class should support the protagonists of this capitalist revolution, simultaneously wresting from them positions of advantage for their future task of opposition and – ultimately – of revolution. It was assumed that there would be a considerable time-lag between the bourgeois revolution and the socialist revolution.

Comrade Trotsky held the view that both revolutions, although they might not coincide, were so inter-connected that we would face a situation of 'permanent revolution'. Starting with a seizure of power by bourgeois political forces, the Russian people would enter a revolutionary period; along with it the rest of the world, too, would not emerge from this period until the total completion of the social revolution. It is undeniable that in formulating these views comrade Trotsky showed great prescience, although his timing was wrong by fifteen years. Incidentally I should point out that in a leading article in *New Life* I also outlined the possibility of a seizure of power by the proletariat and of the retention, under proletarian control, of a form of capitalism which would rapidly evolve towards socialism. I described a situation remarkably similar to our present N.E.P.,[14] but I was given a telling-off by L. B. Krasin[15] who found my article ill-advised and un-Marxist.

The Bolsheviks, with comrade Lenin at their head, were in fact extremely cautious; they held that there were no signs of the proletarian social revolution having begun, but they thought that this revolution had to be encouraged as much as possible without engaging in any theoretical guesswork and prediction, which were foreign to Vladimir Ilyich's nature. In practical terms the Bolsheviks advanced confidently along the correct path. To bring about a plebeian revolution, a revolution similar to the French Revolution that could be taken even further than '93, an alliance with the bourgeoisie was useless: consequently our tactics demanded a break with the bourgeoisie. But we had no intention of isolating the proletariat, for whom we envisaged the enormous task of organizing an alliance with the peasantry, above all with the poor peasantry. Plekhanov was incapable of understanding this. Addressing Lenin he said: 'This new idea of yours sounds a pretty ancient one to me!' Why 'ancient'? Because it seemed to be borrowing the worn-out policy of the S.Rs and to cause us to abandon our characteristic emphasis on the proletariat.

Plekhanov's failure to comprehend our standpoint should not be lightly dismissed as being no more than a typical example of his blinkered super-orthodoxy. Were we not, in the course of our great revolution, once obliged to include some S.Rs, even if left S.Rs, in our government, and was this move entirely free of danger? Are we not delighted now that the childish policies of the left S.Rs themselves have caused their severance from the government? The fears of a 'peasantization' of the Soviet government, of which comrades Shlyapnikov,[16] Kollontai[17] and others occasionally warn us, are unfounded, but the soil which nourishes them is clear to everybody. At the moment it is impossible to say with absolute certainty how a joint workers' and peasants' government will succeed, although everything appears to support comrade Lenin's predictions at the Party Congress that the huge deadweight of the peasantry which, once the plans for a political union of towns and country are completed, will have to be carried with us, is slowing down our movement; but it will never cause us to deviate from the straight and narrow path towards communism.

But all that lay then in the future. At the time, one thing was clear: the workers'-and-peasants' revolution is a proletarian revolution, a bourgeois-and-workers' revolution is a betrayal of the working class. To us this was clear, but not to Plekhanov. I remember that during a very biting speech by Plekhanov my neighbour in the next seat, Alexinsky,[18] then a Bolshevik extremist, nearly boxed his ears but was stopped in time by comrade Sedoi,[19] himself a pretty fiery character, who seized him by the coat-tails. Alas, all that was to end much later in the miserable alliance between Alexinsky and Plekhanov.

It was at the Stockholm Congress that I moved a vote of censure against Plekhanov. My objection amounted to contrasting his view with that of another orthodox theoretician, Kautsky.[20] This was easy, because at that time Kautsky in his pamphlet 'The Motive Force of the Russian Revolution' had shown himself to be in sympathy with us. But Plekhanov was particularly annoyed by my reply to his accusation of Blanquism,[21] when I said that as far as practical notions of making and leading an actual revolution were concerned, he had apparently gathered his ideas from the operetta *Mademoiselle Angot*. In his final rejoinder Plekhanov said some very angry words.

Several more years went by and we met again at the Copenhagen international congress, when our hopes for the first Russian revolution had foundered. I attended the Copenhagen Congress as a representative of the *Forward* group with a consultative vote, but I had practically joined the Bolsheviks and they looked upon me as one of them; indeed they again empowered me to represent them on one of the most important committees – the committee dealing with the cooperatives. The same thing happened here. Plekhanov insisted on the strictest separation of the Party from the cooperatives, fearing contamination by the cooperatives' small-shopkeeper mentality.

I should mention that at the Copenhagen Congress Plekhanov was much closer to the Bolsheviks than to the Mensheviks. As far as I remember Vladimir Ilyich was not too interested in the cooperatives, but nevertheless the Russian delegation listened to my report on the committee and to Plekhanov's objections. Our differences were more or less parallel to those which had arisen between us at Stuttgart on the subject of the trades unions. On this occasion, however, Plekhanov had had little experience of the problem under discussion and there was no particular cause for a clash with him.

In spite of all this, we remained personally on very good terms. He invited me several times to his rooms, we would leave the congress meetings together and he enjoyed giving me his off-the-record impressions of the conference. Plekhanov had by then aged a great deal and was ill, so seriously ill in fact that we were all concerned about him. This did not stop him from being as sharp as ever, and making witty remarks to left and right, strongly biased though they were. He was fondest of all of the old guard. He spoke particularly warmly and graphically of Guesde and of Lafargue,[22] who was already dead. I mentioned Lenin. Here Plekhanov fell silent and he replied to my enthusiasm in terms that were not exactly deprecatory – if anything they were sympathetic – but were somehow vague.

I remember how during a speech by Vandervelde[23] Plekhanov said to me: 'Isn't he exactly like an archdeacon?' His *bon mot* struck me so forcibly that to this day I cannot disentangle the image of an Orthodox deacon chanting the responses from the rhetorical fervour of that famous Belgian. I remember, too, in the course of a speech by Bebel how Plekhanov surprised me by the lapidary precision of his remark: 'Look at that old man – he has exactly the head of Demosthenes.' At once there arose before my mind's eye the famous statue of Demosthenes and the likeness seemed truly striking.

After the Copenhagen Congress I had to read a report

on it at Geneva and at that meeting Plekhanov was my opponent. Later we arranged a few more discussion meetings, sometimes of a philosophical nature (for instance on a lecture by Deborin)[24] and there Plekhanov and I met again. I was extremely fond of having discussions with Plekhanov, despite their complexity and difficulty, but I will refrain from describing them here as I might appear rather one-sided.

After Plekhanov defected from the revolutionary cause, i.e. after his deviation into social-patriotism, I never saw him again.

This is not, I repeat, an attempt to draw a character-sketch of Plekhanov as a man, a thinker or a politician, but it is simply a contribution to the body of literature on Plekhanov drawn from my personal recollections. It may be that they are coloured rather subjectively, but a writer is inevitably subjective. Let the reader accept them as such. No one man, in any case, is capable of encompassing such a great figure with absolute objectivity. That monumental image can ultimately only be recreated from a host of varying opinions. But one thing I can state: Plekhanov and I often clashed, his printed remarks about me were largely negative and hostile, yet in spite of that my memory of Plekhanov is extraordinarily bright, it is a joy to recall those glittering eyes, that astounding intellectual agility, that greatness of spirit or, as Lenin put it, that physical force of his brain, that aristocratic forehead crowning a great democrat. In the final analysis even our great differences, as they are transmuted into the stuff of history, largely drop from the scales whilst the brilliant aspects of Plekhanov's character will endure forever.

In Russian literature Plekhanov stands close to Herzen, in the history of socialism he belongs to that constellation (Kautsky, Lafargue, Guesde, Bebel, old Liebknecht)[25] which revolves round those twin suns, Plekhanov's demigods of whom he – strong, intelligent, incisive and proud as he was – would speak only with the voice of a disciple: Marx and Engels.

Plekhanov was the Grand Old Man of Russian social democracy, the trusted associate of Engels, a thinker of immense erudition and culture, a founder of the Russian social democratic movement and one of the two men (the other was Karl Marx) to whose writings Lenin specifically attributed his own conversion to Marxism. Plekhanov was also rigidly doctrinaire, aloof, an impossible colleague, a man temperamentally unsuited to politics who spent most of his life as a politician. Born in 1857, he joined the Populist revolutionary body 'Land and Freedom' as a young man, but when the group split on the issue of terrorism Plekhanov opted for the non-terrorist faction known as 'The Black Repartition' (i.e. it stood for the re-distribution of the 'black earth' lands among the peasants).

Forced to emigrate to western Europe, Plekhanov became converted to Marxism and was instrumental, by his extraordinarily lucid and tough-minded expositions of Marxism in such works as *Our Differences* and *In Defence of Materialism*, in establishing political Marxism in the minds of a significant handful of intellectuals as the most dynamic, constructive and practical framework for revolution. But he could not for long bear to work with Lenin when it came to putting these theories into harsh practice. Although Plekhanov at first supported Lenin at the notorious Bolshevik–Menshevik split in 1903, he soon veered to Menshevism and thereafter he opposed Lenin on every major issue, although he continued to enjoy an extraordinary degree of respect among the socialist movement. The final breach between the two occurred in Paris in 1914 over their attitudes to the First World War: Lenin wanted Russia to be defeated as the surest way of hastening the collapse of the tsarist regime, whilst Plekhanov revealed the latent streak of emotional Germanophobia that existed in so many socialists of the time and ardently hoped for an Allied victory. This cultured, gentlemanly, essentially bookish man felt so violently about the issue that to another socialist comrade, an 'internationalist', he said: 'So far as I am concerned, if I were not old and sick I would join the army. To bayonet your German comrades would give me great pleasure.'

Soon after the February 1917 revolution Plekhanov hastened back to Russia and organized a right-wing socialist group called 'Unity', but his impact on events was negligible. After the Bolshevik revolution in October/November Plekhanov, then mortally ill with the tuberculosis that had dogged him all his life, was subjected to the most humiliating indignities. On one occasion a band of sailors broke into his house and almost lynched the 'father of Russian Marxism'. His wife, who had been able until then to keep him in some comfort from her earnings as a successful doctor, took him to Finland where he died in May 1918, ignored by Lenin and the triumphant Party Plekhanov had helped to found. Some posthumous amends have, however, been made to Plekhanov's memory: of all the leading Marxists who quarrelled with Lenin, Plekhanov is the only one whose works are still regularly published in the Soviet Union.

1. OUR DIFFERENCES: ('*Nashi Raznoglasiya*'). A polemical tract, published in 1884, in which Plekhanov analysed and stressed the differences in ideology between Marxist and Populist ('Narodnik') socialism.

2. JODKO: Witold Jodko-Narkiewicz (1864–1924). Also known under the pseudonyms of 'A. Wronski' and 'Jowisz' ('Jove'). Polish politician, journalist and diplomat of aristocratic origin and bearing. Supported the Pilsudski-ite right-wing of the Polish Socialist Party (P.P.S.) when the Party split in 1906. 'Defeatist' in the First World War. In 1918 Polish deputy minister of foreign affairs. 1920 – Polish ambassador to Turkey. Died in Warsaw.

3. ROSA LUXEMBURG: Rosa Luxemburg (1871–1919). Born Zamośc̈ in German Poland. Active in the Polish Social Democratic Party, later in the left wing of the German socialist movement. Brilliant journalist and polemicist. Imprisoned in Germany in the First World War for anti-militarism. Founded and published *Die Internationale*, the organ first of the S.P.D. then of German Communist Party (K.P.D.). Arrested and shot on 15 January 1919 in Berlin by the right-wing para-military *Freikorps*.

4. HERZEN MUST HAVE BEEN LIKE THAT: Alexandr Ivanovich Herzen (1812–70). The illegitimate son of a Russian nobleman. Political theorist and publicist, founder of Russian agrarian socialism or Populism. Lived abroad (mostly in London) from 1847, where he published *The Bell*, a very influential Russian *émigré* journal.

5. OLD GREULICH: Hermann Greulich (1842–1925). Right-wing Swiss Social Democrat. Edited various Party journals and held high Party office. Opposed the formation of Third International ('Comintern').

6. AVENARIUS: Richard Avenarius (1843–96). German-Swiss philosopher whose theory of knowledge was known as Empirio-criticism.

7. FICHTE: Johann Gottlieb Fichte (1762–1814). Moral philosopher and preacher of German nationalism.

8. SCHELLING: Friedrich Wilhelm Schelling (1775–1854). German philosopher. Taught the unity of all phenomena.

9. HEGEL: Georg Wilhelm Friedrich Hegel (1770–1831). Hegel's theory of the dialectic process was the foundation of Marx's Dialectical Materialism.

10. D'HOLBACH: Paul Henri, Baron d'Holbach (1723–89). French philosopher and scientist. His strong views on atheism, materialism and determinism were contained in his *Système de la Nature*, published in 1770. Advocated a utilitarian approach to morals and politics in his *Système social* (1773).

11. HELVÉTIUS: Claude Adrien Helvétius (1715–71). His main works, *De l'Esprit* (1758) and *De l'Homme* (1773) contain the exposition of his materialist and hedonist moral philosophy. Man, he taught, is governed entirely by physical sensation, self-interest and passion.

12. DE BROUCKÈRE: Louis De Brouckère (1870–1951). Belgian professor, leading member of the Socialist Labour Party of Belgium. Member of the Executive of the Second International. Later a cabinet minister and delegate to the League of Nations.

13. GUESDE: Jules Basile Guesde (1845–1922). Leading French socialist; at one time headed the left wing of the Party. Deputy from 1893–1921. From August 1914 to October 1915 was Minister without Portfolio in the French cabinet.

14. OUR PRESENT N.E.P.: '*New Economic Policy*'. From 1921–8 the Soviet government's method of restoring Russia's economy by limited incentives to private enterprise in industry and trade, and concessions to the peasants. The N.E.P. was terminated in favour of a totally state-controlled economy when industrial production regained the 1913 level in 1927.

15. L. B. KRASIN: Leonid Borisovich Krasin (1870–1926). Engineer by profession. Elected to the Central Committee of the Social Democratic Party in 1905. Provided the bulk of

Bolshevik funds from his millionaire friend Savva Morozov and by organizing bank raids. In 1908 left revolutionary politics. In 1918 took part in the Brest-Litovsk negotiations. From 1919 first Commissar for Trade, Industry and Transport. Signed the first Anglo-Soviet Trade Treaty, 1921. In 1924 re-elected to the Central Committee of the Party. Sent in 1925 as Soviet ambassador to London, where he died.

16. SHLYAPNIKOV: Alexandr Gavrilovich Shlyapnikov (1883–1943). Metal-worker by trade, joined the Bolsheviks in 1903. After 1905 emigrated to France. From 1915 charged by Lenin with running the Bolshevik Party inside Russia. Took an important part in the Bolshevik *coup* of October 1917. First Soviet Commissar for Labour. Expelled from the Party in 1933, he disappeared in the 'purges' of the thirties.

17. KOLLONTAI: Alexandra Mikhailovna Kollontai (1872–1952). Socialist politician and ardent advocate of 'free love'. A Bolshevik from 1904–5, but later became a Menshevik 'liquidator'. Lived in W. Europe and the U.S.A. from 1908 to 1917, when she returned to Russia and was elected to the Bolshevik Central Committee. From 1923 became a diplomat, representing the U.S.S.R. as ambassador to Norway, Mexico and Sweden until 1945.

18. ALEXINSKY: Grigorii Alexeyevich Alexinsky (b. 1879). Bolshevik deputy to the Second Duma. Parted from Lenin in 1909, joined Bogdanov and Lunacharsky in the *Forward* group. 'Defencist' in the First World War, aligned himself with Plekhanov. After 1917 emigrated to France.

19. SEDOI: Zinovii Yakovlevich Sedoi, alias Litvin (b. 1876). Joined S.D. Party 1897. Underground Party worker till 1905, several times arrested and exiled. Prominent in the armed workers' uprising in the Presnya district, Moscow, 1905. In 1906 emigrated to France, twice arrested for anti-war propaganda. Returned to Russia in 1917. Fought for the Bolsheviks in the Civil War. Elected to the Central Committee of the Party at the Tenth Congress, 1921. From then until 1939 director of a cotton mill.

20. KAUTSKY: Karl Johann Kautsky (1854–1938). Marxist theoretician of German socialism; S.P.D. leader, prominent in Second International. His criticism of Bolshevik Party methods earned him a scathing attack by Lenin in 1918.

21. ACCUSATION OF BLANQUISM: Louis Auguste Blanqui (1805–81). French revolutionary socialist. His advocacy of violent overthrow of the exploiting classes through a small

disciplined conspiratorial Party prefigured Lenin's use of the Bolshevik Party. Blanqui was a leader of the Paris Commune in 1872.

22. LAFARGUE: Paul Lafargue (1842–1911). Karl Marx's son-in-law. French socialist.

23. VANDERVELDE: Emile Vandervelde (1866–1938). Belgian socialist member of parliament, later a cabinet minister. Author of numerous books on socialism.

24. A LECTURE BY DEBORIN: Abram Moiseyevich Deborin (b. 1881). Philosopher and historian. Joined the Bolsheviks in 1903, later joined the Mensheviks. In 1920s was secretary of the History Section of Soviet Academy of Sciences. In 1931 criticized for 'idealism' and faded into obscurity.

25. OLD LIEBKNECHT: Wilhelm Liebknecht (1816–1900). Early German socialist. Father of the better-known Karl Liebknecht, also a socialist leader, who was shot in January 1919 by right-wing forces in Berlin.

YAKOV MIKHAILOVICH SVERDLOV

I first met Yakov Mikhailovich immediately after my return to Russia. Before that I only knew of him from hearsay. I knew that he was a tireless fighter for social democracy, for Bolshevism, knew that he was constantly being sent to prison and into exile, whence he always escaped: whenever they caught him and put him behind bars he would escape again. At once, no matter where fate might take him, he would start organizing Bolshevik committees or cells. Sverdlov in those days was the archetypal Bolshevik underground worker. In that career he acquired two remarkable characteristics which can, I think, be learned nowhere but in an underground movement. The first was an absolutely encyclopaedic knowledge of the entire Party. He appeared to have made a complete study of every one of the tens of thousands of people who made up the Party. His memory contained something like a biographical dictionary of communism.

In every aspect of character which had a bearing on their fitness as revolutionaries Sverdlov could judge people with extraordinary accuracy and finesse. In this he was a real psychologist. He never forgot anything, he knew men's virtues and their achievements, noticed every lapse, every inadequacy. This was the first skill that Sverdlov brought with him from underground Party work. The second was his undoubted organizing ability.

Naturally I cannot say how well Sverdlov would have shown up as an organizer of the day-to-day business of economics and politics once the revolution had turned to the gradual, prosaic realization of our ideals, but as a clandestine operator, in the intensive though limited work of a revolutionary organizer, he was magnificent. This experience clearly equipped Sverdlov well to be the author of our constitution, to make of him an impressive chairman of the C.E.C., combining with this the leadership of the Party secretariat.

Until the July days[1] Sverdlov formed part of the Bolshevik 'general staff', guiding events alongside Lenin, Zinoviev and Stalin. With the July days he was pushed into the limelight. This is not the place to expatiate on the causes or the significance of the July demonstrations of the Petrograd and Kronstadt proletariat. But it is a fact that their technical organization, once it had proved impossible to stop the demonstrations, was largely the work of Sverdlov. It was he who reviewed the gigantic parade of tens of thousands of armed men as they tramped past Kshesinskaya's balcony,[2] he who gave the marching detachments their fighting slogans.

For some strange reason, when the order was issued for the arrest of Lenin and Zinoviev and when Trotsky, myself and many more Bolsheviks and Left S.Rs were put in prison, Sverdlov was not arrested – although the bourgeois Press had directly indicated his leading role in what they called the 'uprising'. At all events this made Sverdlov the effective leader of the Party at that fateful moment, the man who braced its spirit despite the defeats that it had suffered.

Yakov Mikhailovich was raised once more to the crest of history during the convening of the Constituent Assembly.[3] He was appointed its chairman until the election of a presidium.

More than once in these 'profiles' I have had occasion to mention one trait which I have always admired in the leading revolutionaries – their calm, their absolute self-control at moments when to all appearances their nerves should be overstrained, when it seemed impossible to preserve an equilibrium. In Sverdlov, however, this characteristic was not only evident to a most impressive degree, but it seemed to be absolutely natural. I have always thought that both Sverdlov's whole career and his slightly African looks proclaimed an unusually temperamental man. Although there was of course a great deal of inner fire within him, outwardly the man was quite icy. Whenever he was on the rostrum he invariably spoke in a quiet voice, he walked softly, all his gestures were slow as if he were always tacitly saying to those round him: 'Gently, don't hurry; this calls for self-control.'

If Moisei Solomonovich Uritsky, the commissar of the Constituent Assembly, surprised people by his calm during the days of sharp conflict between the Soviet government and the supporters of the Assembly, he appeared positively feverish by comparison with Sverdlov, outwardly so phlegmatic and inwardly so boundlessly confident.

The great majority of Communist and S.R. delegates were agog that day and the whole Tauride Palace was buzzing like an angry swarm: the S.Rs had been spreading rumours that the Bolsheviks were plotting to smash the right wing and centre of the Constituent Assembly, whilst rumours were circulating among the Bolsheviks that the S.Rs had resolved on desperate measures and that besides an armed demonstration – which as we know from the trial[4] was actually in preparation but which never came off – they were going to put up armed resistance to the dispersal of the Constituent Assembly and might attempt in full view of the world and with 'the heroism typical of that party' to assassinate some of the 'usurpers who had brought shame on the revolution' by their 'seizure of the government benches by naked force!'

In fact neither the Bolsheviks nor the S.Rs perpetrated any such excesses and were not even contemplating them. The only difference in the behaviour of the two parties lay in the fact that the Bolsheviks had no need to resort to arms. It was enough for the sailor Zheleznyak[5] to shout, 'Stop chattering and go home!' The S.Rs in general exhibited great 'loyalty', which some of them later bitterly regretted as a clear sign of the cowardice which finally undermined the party's prestige for those who still cherished some illusions about it.

It was in this nervous atmosphere when everybody had taken their seats and when the tension had reached its highest point, that the Right and the Centre were roused to demand the opening of the session. Meanwhile Sverdlov had vanished. Where was he? Some delegates began to grow uneasy. An old greybeard, chosen no doubt because he looked like the oldest member present, was already thundering from the rostrum and stretching out his arm towards the bell. The S.Rs decided to open the session on their own initiative, using one of the proposed elders of the Assembly. But at this moment, without haste and without quickening his step, the figure of Sverdlov emerged as though he had sprung through the floor. With his customary measured gait he advanced to the rostrum, literally disregarding the venerable S.R, removed him, rang the bell and in a voice devoid of the least trace of tension he loudly and with icy calm declared the first session of the Constituent Assembly open.

I mention the details of this scene because psychologically it set the tone for the whole subsequent course of the session. From that moment onward the Left displayed absolute self-control.

The Centre, still seething, seemed to wince and shrivel under this cold douche from Sverdlov. In that chilling tone they felt at once the full steadfastness and decisiveness of the revolutionary government.

I shall not dwell on particular reminiscences of my meetings with Sverdlov nor on my work with him during the first years of the revolution, but I shall merely summarize them.

If the revolution threw up a large number of tireless workers who appeared to exceed the limits of human capacity, then Sverdlov must be placed in the front rank of such men. When he managed to eat and sleep I do not know. He was on duty night and day. Whereas Lenin and a few others provided the intellectual guidance for the revolution, between them and the masses – the Party, the Soviet government apparatus and ultimately all Russia – like a spindle on which it all revolved, like a wire transmitting it all, stood Sverdlov.

At the time, probably instinctively, he adopted a costume which visibly expressed his whole inner personality. He took to wearing leather from head to foot. Firstly he adopted it because it was convenient (he never had time to take it off for long) and secondly he established it, even then, as the commissar's working dress. But that black suit, which shone like the coat of a well-groomed labrador, lent an even greater sense of stature, gravity and solidity to Sverdlov's small, unemphatic figure.

The man was like a diamond, chosen for its absolute hardness to be the axis of some delicate, perpetually revolving piece of mechanism.

The man was like ice; the man was like a diamond. His moral nature, too, had a similar quality that was crystalline, cold and spiky. He was transparently free of personal ambition or any form of personal calculation to such a degree that he was somehow faceless. Nor had he any ideas. He had *orthodox* ideas about everything, but he was only a reflection of the general will, of general Party directives. He never originated anything but merely transmitted what he received from the Central Committee, sometimes from Lenin personally. He transmitted them, of course, clearly and well, adapting them to each concrete situation. When he spoke in public his speeches always bore an official stamp, like leading articles in an official gazette. Everything was carefully thought out; he said what was needed and no more. No sentimentality. No intellectual fireworks. In a given place such and such a statement had to be recorded: it was spoken, noted, ratified and now, he could imply, you may discuss it, make history and so on – the official framework has been laid down.

I cannot say for certain whether our diamond Sverdlov was broken by an excess of work; that is always hard to determine. I think that his doctors underestimated the strain under which a revolutionary lives. I have often heard them say: 'Of course overstrain played a large part in his case, but the root cause of his illness lay elsewhere and would have revealed itself even under the most favourable circumstances, though perhaps somewhat later.' I think they are wrong. I believe that the disease latent in his organism and the external dangers which always surrounded him combined to do him fatal harm only in conjunction with overstrain: this factor was consequently the dominant cause of the catastrophe. Sverdlov caught a cold after one of his speeches in the provinces, but because he refused to give in to it, he actually broke under the weight of the superhuman tasks that he had set himself. For this reason, although unlike some revolutionaries he did not die on the field of battle, we are right to see him as a man who gave his life to the cause he served.

His best epitaph was Lenin's: 'Such men are indispensable. To replace him we need a whole squad of others.'[6]

NOTES

Y. M. Sverdlov (1885–1919) joined the Russian Social Democratic Party in 1901. From 1902 to 1917 he specialized in illegal underground work for Lenin in Russia, having declared himself for the Bolshevik faction from its formation in 1903. Firmly and unquestioningly loyal to Lenin's policies, he was co-opted into the Central Committee in 1913. In 1917, from the February revolution to the Bolshevik *coup* in October he was the Party's indispensable organizer, maintaining continuity of control behind the scenes while Lenin, Zinoviev and other Bolshevik leaders performed on the public stage. After the dissolution of the Constituent Assembly in January 1918, Sverdlov succeeded Kamenev as chairman of the All-Russian Central Executive Committee of the Soviets, an office which made him the titular head of state. From then until his death in March 1919 Sverdlov and Stalin were Lenin's closest collaborators.

1. THE JULY DAYS: A term generally used to refer to the political crisis of mid-July 1917, when a Bolshevik-inspired demonstration, in which Lunacharsky took a leading part, failed to overthrow the Provisional Government. Lenin and Zinoviev fled to Finland.

2. KSHESINSKAYA'S BALCONY: In March 1917 the Bolshevik Party commandeered the palace of Kshesinskaya, a famous ballerina and former mistress of the Tsar, for its Party headquarters in Petrograd.

3. CONSTITUENT ASSEMBLY: Proposed by the Provisional Government, this democratically elected body was to have decided the political future of Russia. Elections to it were

held after the Bolshevik seizure of power in late 1917; the S.R. Party received an absolute majority of votes. When the Assembly refused to be dictated to by the Bolsheviks, the latter forced its dissolution on 18 January 1918 after a session of only one day.

4. AS WE KNOW FROM THE TRIAL: Refers to the show trial of thirty-four members of the Right Socialist Revolutionary Party held in Moscow in April 1922, at which Lunacharsky acted as public prosecutor. Defending counsel included the Belgian Emil Vandervelde. After a completely rigged 'trial', twelve S.Rs were condemned to death, but this was commuted to hard labour as a result of pressure by world public opinion.

5. THE SAILOR ZHELEZNYAK: An Anarchist by political persuasion, Zheleznyakov (Lunacharsky gets his name wrong) commanded the detachment of armed bluejackets placed by the Bolsheviks in the Tauride Palace to 'guard' the delegates to the Constituent Assembly. On Lenin's orders Zheleznyakov dispersed the Assembly.

6. HIS BEST EPITAPH WAS LENIN'S: The lines quoted are a paraphrase of an obituary article written by Lenin in *Pravda* of 20 March 1919.

COMRADE VOLODARSKY

I first met comrade Volodarsky soon after my arrival in Russia.[1]

I stood as a candidate for the Petersburg City Duma and at the elections, in June if I am not mistaken, was elected a councillor. I met Volodarsky at the first meeting of the joint group of the Bolshevik and Interdistrict[2] ('*Mezhraiontsy*') councillors. This joint group, I should mention, contained a fair number of major personalities. Among its members were Kalinin[3] and Joffe[4] and comrades from the Interdistrict party such as Tovbin and Derbyshev; it also included men like comrades Sachs,[5] Axelrod and many others. Yet Volodarsky was in the front rank of that far from mediocre company.

Yakov Mikhailovich Sverdlov, as the 'instructor' of the group, first gave us certain general instructions, after which we began to discuss all the problems which faced us. Volodarsky stood out at once in this discussion. With great shrewdness and mental alacrity he seized on the basic problems of our new task and described how we could combine realistic service to the everyday needs of the working population of Petrograd with the job of revolutionary agitation. I did not then even know Volodarsky's surname. I only saw before me a stocky, well-knit little man with an expressive aquiline profile, clear lively eyes and an incisive diction which reflected his equally clear-cut thinking.

At the break in the session we all went to a café opposite the Duma, where we sat down and continued our discussion. There, involuntarily and somewhat to my own surprise, I said to Volodarsky: 'I'm very glad to see you in our group, because you seem to me to have a perfect grasp of all the complexities of the struggle that faces us everywhere and in the Duma in particular.' Only then did I ask him what his surname was and where he came from. 'My name's Volodarsky,' he replied. 'By origin and upbringing I'm a worker from America. I've been engaged in political agitation for a long time and I've acquired a certain amount of experience.'

Volodarsky very soon gave up Duma work. Before October he emerged as one of the Party's most powerful agitators, even when compared with the hectic and sometimes flamboyant efforts of such propagandists as Trotsky, Zinoviev and others.

It was, however, after October that Volodarsky really came into his own. Then his personality made him to some degree the most striking representative of our party in Petrograd. He owed his position to his outstanding talent as an agitator, to his courageous rectitude, his absolutely superhuman capacity for work and finally to the fact that he combined truly colossal achievements as a speaker with his exemplary work as editor of the *Red Gazette*.

I shall try first to give an approximate picture of Volodarsky as a public speaker and an agitator.

From a literary stand-point Volodarsky's speeches were not remarkable for originality of form or for that richness of metaphor with which Trotsky regaled his audiences in superabundance. In this respect Volodarsky's speeches were on the dry side. They would have delighted our present-day Constructivists[6] – if only, though, they were genuine Constructivists and not such woolly-minded dunces. His speeches were like a machine: there was nothing superfluous, every component meshed in with the next, everything was metallic glitter, everything throbbed with an inner charge of electricity. Perhaps this was the American style of eloquence; but America, which sent back to us so many Russians who had been through her iron school, produced no other orator to compare with Volodarsky.

His voice seemed to print the words – it had a graphic poster-like quality with a metallic ring to it. The sentences flowed remarkably evenly and with an unvarying pressure which was only occasionally heightened. In its clarity and regularity the rhythm of his speech reminded me more than anything else of Mayakovsky's style of declamation.

A kind of revolutionary incandescence burned within him. Behind that brilliant and apparently machine-like drive one could sense his bubbling enthusiasm and the agony of his proletarian heart. His speeches were spell-binding. They were not long, they were unusually easy to understand, each one a whole armoury of slogans, of sharp well-aimed verbal shafts.

He seemed to forge the hearts of his listeners. Listening to him one realized, more than with any other orator, how an agitator, in this age when political agitation has flourished as perhaps never before, could knead the dough of humankind until it took shape under his hands and was transformed into the essential weapon of revolution.

Volodarsky's rhetorical gifts were his greatest, but this was by no means all. He was also a first-class managing editor and in his way indispensable as a journalist. His *Red Gazette* immediately became a really fighting newspaper, the house-journal of the revolution, easily understood by the masses, even more so than *Pravda*, for all the universality of its appeal. His whole newspaper reflected the man himself – sensible, put together with all his American know-how and outstanding in its avoidance of the superfluous, simple and in its simplicity powerfully effective. He wrote as he spoke, with remarkable ease. He never strove after great originality. He aimed his articles as he did his words, like bullets. Nobody, when they fire a volley and attack, bothers whether the bullets are original or not. Yet his bullet-like words, spoken and printed, riddled every obstacle.

In whatever he did, Volodarsky was a good organizer. With the same ease and instinctive skill with which he could drum up an impromptu speech on any subject and cause a crowd to gather round him, he could, I believe, have run any organization. But he was never able to demonstrate the full scope of his organizing ability as he was killed so soon and before he died we were only able to use his administrative gifts on the *Red Gazette* and as chief of the Press Division of the erstwhile Executive Committee of the Union of Northern Communes. As a 'censor' the bourgeoisie cordially detested him.

The bourgeoisie and all its hangers-on hated him, too, as a politician. I do not think they hated any of us as much as him. He was also secretly loathed by the S.Rs. Why this detestation of Volodarsky? Firstly because he was ubiquitous: he flew from meeting to meeting and he was to be seen both in Petersburg and in the outlying districts practically simultaneously. The workers came to treat him as a living newspaper. And he was ruthless. He was imbued not only with the full menace of the October Revolution, but with a foretaste of the outbursts of Red terror which were to come after his death. There is no sense in concealing the fact that Volodarsky was a terrorist. He was profoundly convinced that if we were to falter in lashing out at the hydra of counter-revolution it would devour not only us but along with us the hopes that October had raised all over the world.

He was an absolutely dedicated fighter, ready to go wherever he was needed. There was something of Marat in his ruthlessness, but unlike Marat he sought the light of day: not for him the role of hidden counsellor, of *éminence grise*. He was, on the contrary, always on view with his aquiline beak and his vigilant stare, always in full voice with that special rasp in his throat, always to be seen in the front row, a target for his enemies, the on-the-spot leader.

So they killed him.

Looking back one realizes that it was bound to happen. Petersburg at the time was governed by Zinoviev. His enemies could not tolerate him and they would probably have killed him too if a suitable chance had arisen. The iron hand, who kept a firm grip on the throat of counter-revolution, was Uritsky and he too was soon killed. But it was Volodarsky who was our standard-bearer, our drummer, our trumpeter. He marched ahead not like a general but like a great drum-major in front of a titanic column. Many fell at that time, but they fell in open fight. Volodarsky was the first to be stricken by a murderer's bullet. We all realized that the S.Rs had done it, as was later proved to be the case. They were, after all, the most resolute section of the bourgeoisie.

But it was not a bourgeois hand which cut down Volodarsky, the dedicated tribune of the people, the *chevalier sans peur* of the proletarian order. Yes, he was laid low by the hand of a worker. His murderer was a sickly little workman, a great idealist. For years this mild, hollow-chested man had dreamed of how he could serve the revolution of his class, serve the cause and if need be die a martyr's death. And then along came the intellectuals, who had done penal servitude in Siberia, men who had earned the right, so to speak, to decorate their chests with revolutionary medals.

Inwardly these intellectuals accepted the revolution as their own cause, the cause that would bring them, the advance guard of the petty bourgeoisie, to power. These intellectuals were already in their Millerand Armchairs,[7] they had already come to terms with the bourgeoisie, had already tasted the sweetness of being the henchmen of capitalism and using the gilded pink screen of their revolutionary phrases to protect capitalism from the fury of the rising proletariat. But now the people's tribunes had arisen to lead those angry men forward, to rip down the pink gilded screen, overturn the ministerial seats of these highly respected Chernovs and Tseretellis[8] and sweep away with an iron hand the intellectuals' heroes and their hopes, along with all those capitalists who had hurriedly adapted themselves to the new order of things.

Oh, what hatred, what heroic pathos dripping with the sentimentality of hollow phrasemaking burned in the breasts of those jilted newlyweds of the revolution! And those intellectuals, exploiting the trust of the little hollow-chested workman said to him: 'Do you want to strike a blow in the name of your class, are you prepared for a martyr's death? Then go and kill Volodarsky. We're not ordering you to do it: we'll choose the moment, we must still work out the means, but one thing only we can promise you – it will be a feat worth dying for.'

So having supplied the wretched man with a gun and subjected him to the mental strain of preparing to assassinate a tribune beloved of his people, the gentlemen of the S.R party let day drag after day, week after week while they stalked Volodarsky like a marked beast. But of course the murderer had quite another reason for being in an open space where Volodarsky's car was due to pass by! But of course the S.Rs were innocent of the murder because they hadn't meant the assassin to pull the trigger at that particular moment! He pulled it simply because the car burst a tyre and the murderer thought it a suitable occasion to shoot Volodarsky. And he did so. The S.Rs were not only embarrassed, they were indignant and at once announced in their newspaper that they had nothing to do with it.

It is worth recalling the circumstances that surrounded Volodarsky's murder. On the day of his death he had telephoned Zinoviev to say that he was at the Obukhovsky works and that there was a great deal of unrest at that factory, then under semi-proletarian control, where there were obvious signs of anti-semitism, reckless hooliganism and petty-bourgeois reaction.

This was the time when the S.Rs – hand-in-glove with the officers of the Naval Mines Division – had incited the lower deck of the Mines Division[9] so successfully that at a meeting where Raskolnikov[10] and I were speaking the duped sailors from the minelayers chorused the slogan: 'Russia needs the dictatorship of the Baltic Fleet.' Nobody raised an objection when we pointed out that behind that dictatorship stood the dictatorship of a few officers who had been greased with liquid S.R-ism and a few even obscurer individuals whose connections, via the ironically smiling Admiral Shchastny,[11] extended to the black depths of the pit. The Mines Division was behind the unrest at the Obukhovsky works.

Volodarsky asked Zinoviev to go to the Obukhovsky works and to try and quell the trouble with his personal authority. Zinoviev asked me to go with him and for two hours, amid the shouts and boos of the S.R. and Menshevist rabble (all the reactionary elements at the factory were traced back to the S.Rs and the Mensheviks) we tried to bring the excited mob to order. On our way back from the Obukhovsky works, before we had reached the Neva check-point, we learned that Volodarsky had been killed.

Grief and horror seized the working-class population. The bullet which killed Volodarsky also put an end to the whole Obukhovsky–Mines Division plot. The Petersburg Executive Committee disarmed the Mines Division and the uproar at the Obukhovsky works was immediately stilled.

In the Great Catherine Hall of the Tauride Palace, drowning in a sea of flowers, palm leaves and red ribbons, lay Volodarsky, the stricken eagle. His proud features jutted forth more sharply than ever, like a Roman emperor in bronze. Silent, he still commanded respect. His lips, from which in his time had flowed such fervent, hard-hitting speeches, were compressed as though conscious that he had said all he had to say. I was deeply impressed by the attitude of some old working-class women to the dead man. I saw several of them approach with a mother's tears in their eyes, gaze long and lovingly at the murdered hero and say with convulsive sobs: 'Our darling one.'

Volodarsky's funeral cortège was one of the most majestic that Petersburg, no stranger to great events, has ever seen. Tens, perhaps hundreds of thousands of work-people followed him to his grave on the Field of Mars. What did his S.R. murderers feel then? Did they know against whom they had raised their hand? Did they admit to themselves how at heart the *entire* Petersburg proletariat was on his side, on ours, the side of the Communist Party? They did not. Their only aim had been to point their revolver. They had canvassed obliging terrorists to see how suitable some new Konoplyova, some new Kaplan[12] might be for 'new deeds and new victims'.

The hatred of Volodarsky was such that the temporary monument to him erected not far from the Winter Palace was blown up when Yudenich[13] was advancing on Petersburg. On my last visit to Petersburg I saw that monument battered and partly mutilated in the hallway of the Museum of the Revolution. I cannot say that the artist made a very good job of the monument. It will in any case have to be changed later for one that is more solid and more artistic.[14] But such as he is, that grey giant with his aquiline features, battered and splintered below, stares proudly into the future with victory on his brow.

'Volodarsky' was the Party alias of Moisei Markovich Goldstein (1891–1918). Born in a poor Jewish family in Volhynia (W. Ukraine), he was exiled to Archangel while still a schoolboy for 'political unreliability'. In 1905 he joined the *Bund*, later the '*Spilka*' or Ukrainian S.R. Party. Arrested in 1911, he was again sent to Archangel. After the 1913 general amnesty Goldstein emigrated to the U.S.A., where he worked as a tailor in a Philadelphia sweat-shop. This led him into the American Socialist Party and the International Garment Workers' Union. During the First World War he joined Bukharin and Trotsky in New York where they edited the Russian-language socialist paper *New World*. In 1917 Goldstein (now Volodarsky) went back to Petrograd in May and plunged into active Bolshevik politics. Driving from one workers' meeting to another, Volodarsky was shot on 20 June 1918 in Farforov Street by Sergeyev, a Right S.R.

1. MY ARRIVAL IN RUSSIA: Refers to Lunacharsky's return to Russia from Switzerland in April 1917.

2. INTERDISTRICT: Shortened name of the '*Interdistrict Organization of United Social Democrats*', a left-of-centre non-factional Social Democratic grouping founded in 1913 by K. K. Yurenev. Politically very influential, despite its numerical weakness compared with Bolsheviks and Mensheviks, its members included Trotsky, Lunacharsky and Volodarsky. At the Sixth Congress of the Bolshevik Party in July 1917 the 'Interdistrict' members *en bloc* joined the Bolsheviks.

3. KALININ: Mikhail Ivanovich Kalinin (1875–1946). A metalworker of peasant origin, became a Social Democrat in 1897. Elected to the Bolshevik Central Committee in 1919, to the Politburo in 1926. Titular head of the Soviet state from 1919 until his death.

4. JOFFE: Adolf Joffe, alias V. Krymsky (1883–1927). (Sometimes spelled 'Yoffe'.) Early Social Democrat. First a Menshevik, then like Lunacharsky a 'Forwardist', later joined 'Interdistrict'. Close personal friend of Trotsky. Delegate at the Brest-Litovsk peace negotiations. Later Soviet ambassador to China, Japan and Austria. On hearing of Trotsky's banishment to Central Asia in 1927, Joffe committed suicide.

5. SACHS: G. D. Sachs (b. 1882). Early member of the Socialist Revolutionary Party. Elected to Party Central Committee in 1905. Became a Left S.R. when the Party split in 1917. Member of the Military Revolutionary Committee which organized the Bolshevik seizure of power in October 1917. Joined the Bolsheviks after the Left S.Rs' revolt in 1918.

6. OUR . . . CONSTRUCTIVISTS: An avant-garde movement of the twenties in art, architecture and stage production. Main proponent was Vladimir Tatlin, who used 'industrial' materials – wire, glass, sheet metal – to define and articulate spatial relationships. In the theatre this technique was used in stage design by Taïrov and Meyerhold, the latter extending the formal deployment of abstract line, planes and levels to an altogether anti-realistic style of acting devoid of all emotion and illusion. It is to this latter aspect of Constructivism that Lunacharsky sarcastically refers; himself a playwright, Lunacharsky was a traditionalist in stage technique.

7. MILLERAND ARMCHAIRS: Alexandre Millerand (1859–1943). French socialist politician. Originally the leader of left-wing socialism, he was bitterly denounced by many fellow-socialists for accepting a cabinet post in 1899. He incurred even greater left-wing odium for his tenure of office as minister of war from 1912 to 1915. The Soviet leaders particularly detested Millerand for supplying arms to Poland in the Russo-Polish War of 1920. From 1920 to 1924 President of the French Republic. Referring to the Right S.Rs, Lunacharsky here uses Millerand's name as a term of abuse to typify all 'renegade' socialists.

8. TSERETELLIS: Irakli Tseretelli (1881–1959). Georgian Social Democrat. Menshevik deputy to the Second Duma. Sentenced to hard labour in 1907, exiled to Siberia from 1912 to 1917. Member of several coalition cabinets of the Provisional Government. Emigrated after the Bolshevik *coup* in 1917.

9. LOWER DECK OF THE MINES DIVISION: Throughout the 1917 revolutions and their aftermath, the Russian naval ratings of all ranks were extremely militant. There was, however, a significant ideological difference between the crews of the large capital ships based at Kronstadt, who tended to be Bolshevist or Anarchist, and the crews of the smaller craft based at Petrograd (e.g. minelayers and submarines) whose sympathies were more with the S.Rs.

10. RASKOLNIKOV: F. F. Ilyin, alias Raskolnikov (1892–1939). Joined Social Democratic Party in 1910. Enlisted in the tsarist Navy in 1914. Led the Bolshevik group of the Kronstadt sailors in 1917. Chairman of the Kronstadt Soviet.

11. ADMIRAL SCHASTNY: In September 1917 Finland, under German influence, declared herself independent of Russia. Schastny at once ordered all Russian warships in Helsinki harbour to steam to Kronstadt. This timely move saved a considerable portion of the Baltic Fleet from falling into German hands. Although Lenin welcomed his action, Schastny was regarded by Trotsky as politically unreliable, charged with spreading anti-Bolshevik propaganda and shot.

12. KAPLAN: Fanny Kaplan. Woman terrorist who shot at and gravely injured Lenin in Moscow on 30 August 1918, the same day on which Uritsky was assassinated in Petrograd. A one-time Anarchist, Fanny Kaplan was mentally unbalanced as a result of imprisonment for terrorism under the tsarist regime. Lunacharsky implies that she was a hireling or adherent of the S.Rs, but no evidence of such was ever produced. She was shot without trial. These two nearly simultaneous attacks on Bolshevik leaders unleashed a wave of terror against all actual or imagined 'counter-revolutionaries'.

13. YUDENICH: Nikolai Nikolaievich Yudenich (1862–1933). Russian general. As the senior officer in the area, Yudenich took command of the 'White' Russian forces in Esthonia, the most northerly of the three Baltic states. Entirely lacking in political sense, Yudenich antagonized the Esthonians, on whom he relied for support. However, twice in 1919, in May and September, his troops almost took Petrograd from the Reds, but the final advance petered out in the city's outskirts.

14. MORE SOLID AND MORE ARTISTIC: The damaged monument was replaced by a plain granite obelisk on a square granite plinth at the site of the murder, without head or bust of Volodarsky but inscribed: 'Here on 20 June 1918 a hired assassin treacherously shot the beloved leader of the Petersburg workers V. Volodarsky.'

MOISEI SOLOMONOVICH URITSKY

My acquaintance with him began in 1901.

Between prison and exile I was released for a short period to see relatives in Kiev.

At the request of the local 'Political Red Cross'[1] I gave a lecture on its behalf. All of us – lecturer and audience, which included E. Tarlé[2] and V. Vodovozov[3] – were taken under cossack escort to the Lukyanovsky prison.

When we had looked around a little we realized that this was rather a special prison: the cell doors were never locked, exercise was taken communally and during exercise we sometimes played games, sometimes attended lectures on scientific socialism. At night we all sat at the windows and the singing and recitations would begin. The prison was run as a Commune, so that both the prison rations and the parcels sent by our families all went into the common pot. The Commune of political prisoners was allowed to go shopping in the market, for which we pooled our resources; we also ran the kitchen, which was fully staffed by the criminal inmates. The criminals regarded the Commune with adoration, as it was ultimately the reason why the prisoners were not beaten-up or even sworn at.

What miracle had turned the Lukyanovsky detainees into a Commune? It was because the prison was run less by its governor than by the senior 'political' – Moisei Solomonovich Uritsky.

In those days he wore a large black beard and sucked perpetually at a small pipe. Phlegmatic, imperturbable as a sea-going bo'sun, he strode about the prison with his characteristic bear-like gait. He knew everything, found his way everywhere, impressed everybody and was kind to some, harsh to others, his authority challenged by none.

He dominated the prison staff by his calm strength and put his moral superiority to powerful and effective use.

Years passed in which we were both exiled, both became *émigrés*.

Moisei Solomonovich Uritsky, a Left Menshevik, was a sincere and ardent revolutionary and a socialist. Beneath his apparent coldness and phlegm there was concealed a titanic faith in the cause of the working class.

He made fun of all those eloquent speeches full of pathos about the great and beautiful; he was proud of being level-headed and was fond of making play with it, even to the point of apparent cynicism, but in fact he was an idealist of the purest water. For him, life outside the workers' movement did not exist. His enormous political passion did not seethe or bubble – simply because it was methodically and systematically directed to one end. He therefore expressed it only in action – highly effective action.

His logic was inflexible. The 1914 war set him on the course of internationalism and he sought no middle way. Like Trotsky, like Chicherin,[4] like Joffe, he soon realized the utter impossibility of maintaining even the shadow of a link with the Menshevik Defencists and he therefore broke radically with the Martov group, who could not understand why he did so.

Even before the war, along with the man who stood politically closest to him, L. D. Trotsky, he was closer to the Bolsheviks than to the Mensheviks.

After a long separation I met him again in Berlin in 1913. The same story happened again! I have always been unlucky when lecturing. The Russian colony in Berlin invited me to give two lectures, but the Berlin police arrested me, held me in prison for a short spell and expelled me from Prussia without right of re-entry. Again Uritsky appeared like a good genie. He not only spoke excellent German but had connections everywhere which he set in motion to convert my arrest into a major scandal for the government. Once more I admired how, smiling ironically, he would talk to a detective or to bourgeois journalists and how he described our campaign at a consultation with Karl Liebknecht, who had also taken an interest in this minor but significant incident.

And always there was that same impression of unruffled confidence and an amazing talent for organization.

During the war Uritsky, living in Copenhagen, did important work there too. But his great organizing abilities gradually developed to colossal proportions in Russia itself during our glorious revolution.

At first he joined the so-called Interdistrict organization. He pulled it into shape and the arrangements for its complete and unconditional fusion with the Bolsheviks was to a great degree due to him.

As the 25th October drew closer Uritsky's strength came to be increasingly appreciated at the Bolshevik headquarters.

By no means everyone is aware of the truly gigantic role played in Petrograd by the Military Revolutionary Committee,[5] beginning on about the 20th October and lasting until the middle of November. The culmination of this superhuman organizational effort were the days and nights from the 24th to the end of the month. Throughout those days and nights Moisei Solomonovich never slept. Round him was a handful of men of great strength and stamina, but they became exhausted, were relieved, took turns at the work: Uritsky, his eyes red with lack of sleep, but as calm and smiling as ever, stayed at his post in the armchair where all the threads met and whence were issued all the directives of that makeshift, crude but mighty revolutionary organization.

At the time I regarded Moisei Solomonovich's contribution as an absolute marvel of efficiency, self-discipline and skill. I still consider this page of his life's work to have been a miracle of its kind. But that page was not the last and even that brilliant episode has not overshadowed his subsequent achievements.

After the victory of the 25th October and the series of victories which succeeded it all over Russia, one of the most anxious moments was the problem of how relations would develop between the Soviet government and the impending Constituent Assembly. The settlement of this question demanded a politician of the first rank who would be capable of combining an iron will with the necessary tactical skill. No more than one name was ever put forward: Uritsky's candidature was instantly and unanimously approved.

What a sight it was to have seen our 'Commissar of the Constituent Assembly' during those stormy days! I can understand how all those 'democrats', mouthing their magnificent phrases about justice, freedom and so on, burned with hatred for the chubby little man who watched them through the round black frames of his *pince-nez* with such frigid irony and who shattered all their illusions with nothing more than his sobering smile, his every gesture embodying the ascendancy of revolutionary force over revolutionary phrase-mongering!

When on the first and last day of the Constituent Assembly Chernov's solemn speeches rolled over the turbulent sea of S.Rs and the 'sovereign assembly' tried at every turn to prove that it and no other was the real government, comrade Uritsky paced the Tauride Palace exactly as he had once prowled about the Lukyanovsky prison, with that same bear's gait, with the same smiling imperturbability and once again he knew everything, found his way everywhere, inspiring some with calm confidence, others with utter despair.

'There's something fateful about Uritsky!' I heard one Right S.R. say in the corridors on that memorable day.

The Constituent Assembly was liquidated. But a new and even more disturbing problem was to arise – Brest-Litovsk.

Uritsky was an ardent opponent of peace with Germany. This man, the very incarnation of coolness, said with his usual smile: 'Would it not be better to die with honour?' Yet when certain left-wing Communists showed signs of losing their nerve M.S. replied calmly: 'Party discipline above all!' And for him that was no empty phrase.

The German February offensive was unleashed.

Forced to leave, the Council of People's Commissars laid the responsibility for Petrograd, which was in an almost desperate position, on the shoulders of comrade Zinoviev.

'It will be very hard,' said Lenin to those who were left behind, 'but Uritsky is staying' – and this calmed them.

Then began Moisei Solomonovich's skilful and heroic struggle against counter-revolution and the black market in Petrograd.

What curses, what accusations were heaped on him! Yes, he was ferocious: he reduced them to despair by his implacability, by his vigilance. Combining the joint control of the Extraordinary Commission[6] and the Commissariat of Internal Affairs and to a large extent the guidance of foreign policy, he was the most terrible foe in Petrograd of the thieves and robbers of imperialism of all colours and all varieties.

They knew what a powerful enemy he was. He was hated, too, by the petty-bourgeoisie who saw in him the incarnation of Bolshevist terror.

But we, we who stood shoulder to shoulder with him, we knew how much generosity of heart there was in him and how he was able to combine a necessary harshness with genuine goodness. Of course there was not a drop of sentimentality in his make-up but there was much kindness too. We know that his work was as agonizing as it was hard and thankless.

Moisei Solomonovich suffered a great deal in his task, but we never once heard this strong man complain. Totally disciplined, he was the absolute embodiment of revolutionary duty.

They killed him. They struck us a truly well-aimed blow. They picked out one of the most gifted and powerful of their enemies, one of the most gifted and powerful champions of the working class.

To have killed Lenin and Uritsky would have meant more than winning a resounding victory at the front.

It will be hard to close our ranks: a tremendous breach has been made in them. But Lenin is recovering* and we must do our utmost to replace the unforgettable and irreplaceable Moisei Solomonovich Uritsky – by each one of us increasing his efforts tenfold.

* This article was written after Vladimir Ilyich had been wounded.

Uritsky was born in 1873, son of a Jewish businessman. During his law studies at Kiev University he joined the Social Democratic Party and organized a network for importing and distributing political literature. In 1897 came arrest and exile for running an illegal mimeograph press. At the Party split in 1903 Uritsky sided with the Mensheviks; his activities in Petersburg during the 1905 revolution earned him a further term of exile. In 1914 he emigrated to France and contributed to the Party newspaper *Our Word.* Back in Russia in 1917 he made the familiar progression via 'Interdistrict' membership to the Bolshevik Party, to whose Central Committee he was elected in July 1917. Uritsky played a leading part in the Bolsheviks' armed take-over in October. Appointed chairman of the Petrograd *Cheka* (secret police) in 1918, Uritsky was shot on 30 August by an S.R. named Kannegiesser.

1. LOCAL 'POLITICAL RED CROSS': A rare example of collaboration between the revolutionary parties of all shades under the tsarist regime, the *Political Red Cross* was a non-affiliated underground organization which gave legal and material aid to political detainees of all allegiances.

2. TARLÉ: E. V. Tarlé (1875–1955). Russian historian. Politically a liberal until 1917, he accepted the Bolshevik regime and, despite vicissitudes, survived to become a member of the Academy of Sciences. Widely known for his works on Napoleon and Talleyrand.

3. VODOVOZOV: V. V. Vodovozov (1864–1933). Economist and journalist, theoretician of Populism.

4. CHICHERIN: Georgii Vasilievich Chicherin (1872–1936). Began his career as a civil servant in the tsarist Foreign Ministry. In 1904 emigrated to Berlin, where he became a Menshevik Social Democrat, thereafter worked mostly abroad in the labour movements of Germany, France and England. Declaring allegiance to the Bolsheviks in 1917, Chicherin was imprisoned in Brixton jail for enemy sympathies. Released in 1918 in exchange for Sir George Buchanan, last British ambassador to the old regime. Commissar for Foreign Affairs, negotiated the Rapallo Treaty with Germany in 1922. Resigned for health reasons in 1930.

5. MILITARY REVOLUTIONARY COMMITTEE: The Bolshevik-organized body, led by Trotsky but including a number of militant Left Mensheviks and Left S.Rs, which actually organized and staged the armed *coup* of October 1917. Having physically deposed the Provisional Government, the M.R.C. temporarily assumed sovereignty over Russia, nominally on behalf of the Petrograd Soviet, in fact on behalf of Lenin and the Bolshevik Party.

6. EXTRAORDINARY COMMISSION: Abbreviated title of the *Extraordinary Commission for Combating Counter-revolution, Speculation and Delinquency in Office*, or secret police. Widely known as the CHEKA, an abbreviation derived from the cyrillic initial letters (ЧК) of the Russian words for 'Extraordinary Commission'. Formed on 20 December 1917 as a Bolshevik Party organ and headed by Felix Edmundovich Dzerzhinsky (1877–1926), a Pole of aristocratic origin, member of the Party Central Committee. The CHEKA soon developed into the State security force, extant to this day, which has acquired notoriety under its various titles such as O.G.P.U., N.K.V.D., M.V.D., M.G.B., K.G.B. Its present head (March 1967) is Vladimir Semichastny.

YULII OSIPOVICH MARTOV (TSEDERBAUM)

I first heard of Martov as one of the three inseparable persons of the trinity – Lenin, Martov, Potresov. These were the three Russian social democrats who breathed new life into the *émigré* social-democratic general staff which had created *The Spark*.

When I arrived in Paris on the way to Geneva where I was to join the Bolsheviks' central editorial staff, I met there O. N. Chernosvitova, who was related to me by marriage and who knew Martov well. She spoke enthusiastically of him as a man fascinating in the breadth of his interests.

'I am sure,' she said to me, 'that you and Martov will become very close friends. He's not like the other social democrats, who are all so blinkered and fanatical. Martov's mind is wide-ranging and flexible and nothing is beneath his interest.' This description certainly disposed me very well towards Martov, although a political gulf divided us at the time.

My first actual meeting with Martov could hardly have been less propitious. The Mensheviks had tried to stir up some nasty little scandal during one of my lectures by shouting, causing a disturbance and trying to break up the meeting. There occurred a sharp clash between Martov and my wife. First Lyadov and then I intervened and some sharp words passed between us.

Despite the unpleasantness of our initial encounter, relations between us were never really hostile. During my stay in Switzerland we seldom met and in general Bolsheviks and Mensheviks lived completely separate lives. We only met, one might say, on the field of battle, i.e. at meetings and discussions, but news of each other naturally passed to and fro. I came to regard Martov as a rather charming type of bohemian with something of the eternal student about his appearance, by predilection a haunter of cafés, indifferent to comfort, perpetually arguing and a bit of an eccentric.

This impression, of Martov's outward characteristics at least, was confirmed when I later came to know him very much better. I shall now attempt to describe Martov in greater detail as a writer and speaker during his Swiss period.

Outwardly Martov was a boring lecturer. He had a weak voice, a peculiar toneless and abrupt way of ending every sentence as though he were biting it off. His puny frame, combined with his *pince-nez* drooping slightly on his large nose, seemed so typical of the theorizing intellectual that there was no question of him being the kind of popular tribune who could kindle an audience. Sometimes, when Martov appeared on the platform when he was tired, his voice dropped until it was barely intelligible and his speech became an affair of deadly boredom. Furthermore Martov could hardly ever speak briefly: as an orator he needed, as it were, to spread his elbows on the desk. This made his speeches at times grey and monotonous despite the fact that they never lacked content.

If one could only follow the thread of Martov's thought during his dreary lectures, there was always something valuable to be gained from them. But he also had his moments of brilliance. Most of all he warmed up in the cut and thrust of polemical argument and for this reason Martov was at his most effective when speaking impromptu, during the dialogue with his opponents after a lecture and in his summing-up. I know many masters of the spoken word who are at their most dangerous when summing up. Plekhanov could be caustic and brilliant, but he nevertheless disdained to exploit all the advantages of the final summing-up, to which there is no reply. He was even skilled enough to recapitulate, crush and destroy any objections put forward by Vladimir Ilyich as though they were so many trifling irrelevancies, yet I know of no one who can beat Martov at this game. If Martov has the last word, you can never feel sure of yourself, however convinced you may be of the rightness of your cause, however well armed you may be.

Martov always comes to life during a summing-up; he overflows with irony, his subtle mind flashes with real brilliance, he can dissect everything that his opponent has said and exploit absolutely every loophole and the least deviation. He is a supremely gifted analyst and if there be the tiniest chink in your armour you may be sure that it will be precisely there that Martov's unerring blade will pierce you. As he does so he will grow livelier and livelier and make the audience laugh or move them to murmurs of protest.

Martov behaves similarly whenever he speaks on some subject which particularly excites him, which frequently happened during the tragic days of our revolution. Some of his speeches in the Petrograd Soviet during its Menshevist period, at separate meetings of the Mensheviks and at plenary meetings of the Soviet delegates, speeches chiefly right-wing in tendency, were truly superb, not only in content but in the fervour of his indignation and his honourable, sincere expression of revolutionary feeling. I remember how Martov, after a speech in support of Grimm[1] against Tseretelli, made even Trotsky exclaim: 'Long live the honest revolutionary Martov!'

When discussing men like Lenin, Trotsky and Zinoviev, one cannot help remarking on their greater strength as orators than as writers, although all three of these leaders of the Russian revolution are greater masters of the pen. With Martov the reverse is true. As a speaker he is only successful in bursts, in fits and starts when he is on form and even then the superficial effectiveness of his performance is inclined to overshadow his expertise in the speech's construction and the profundity of his thought. All this, however, comes to the fore in Martov's articles. As a writer Martov's style is extraordinarily noble. He does not care to lard his written language with little witticisms or embellish it with all kinds of images and figures of speech. On the page Martov's writing lacks immediate brilliance because it has no pattern. At the same time, however, it does not have that special crude simplicity, that distinctive vulgarization of form without vulgarization of thought which is the strength of that genuinely popular leader,

Lenin. Martov seems to write in language that is slightly monotonous yet sensitive and movingly sincere, which clothes the thought as though with the graceful folds of a Greek chiton and which allows his thought to stand out in all the elegant proportions of its logical structure. Essentially, however, Martov is not a thinker; he is fundamentally incapable of generating any original ideas. To speak of Martov as a thinker – one cannot begin to compare him with Marx, but compared with, say, Kautsky – is simply impossible. In the sphere of revolutionary tactics the cyclopean armoury of someone like Lenin is crushingly superior to Martov's subtle constructs. No, it is not a question of his ability to coin effective slogans or of the breadth of his grasp of revolutionary technique, but rather of his extraordinary gift of precise analysis, his ability to work with a magnifying glass and to mint the coinage of his thought. Martov's intellect is an instrument for polishing and refining. His tactical or political ideas always have a finished look, honed down until his chosen theme stands out with total clarity.

As a politician Martov starts with certain fundamental handicaps. He has neither the temperament, the boldness nor the breadth of vision needed for a political leader. He loses himself in matters of detail and is naturally inclined to that circumspection and caution which develops into timidity and dilutes the revolutionary urge. Of those who suffer from this, some end up as bourgeois philistines, others as mere armchair revolutionaries. Martov undoubtedly has some of the characteristics of an armchair politician. I will go further and say that Martov puts his incomparable political gifts and his persuasive journalistic ability largely at the service of other people's ideas. Martov is an excellent ideological costumier: with great taste he cuts and sews a beautifully fitting ideological garment to clothe the slogans which the more determined Mensheviks have worked out behind his back. Even indecision needs a certain decisiveness. In the case of the typical dyed-in-the-wool Mensheviks, their political vacillation does not stem from a lack of strength of character – personally they may be extremely tough and authoritative

– it stems from the class interests of middle-of-the-road factions. Such midway groups are indecisive by their very nature. They are doomed to be thrust by history into the middle ground between irreconcilable classes, hence the total lack of anything remotely heroic about their posture. But these men are sometimes capable of implementing their compromise decisions with great firmness and, since in a revolutionary situation they represent the last hope of the extremely cunning and still influential grouping of the privileged classes, they become at times, like Noske,[2] men who will lend an iron hand to the service of the quasi-enemies of their class in overcoming their brothers of the left, whilst their own leftism dissolves into mere revolutionary phrases serving to screen their real activities – which at times extend to repression.

Martov is incapable of such a role, but his inherently miniaturist style, his whole cast of mind which tends to treat facts in isolation and is incapable of tolerating those harsh, sharp lines which revolutionary passion slashes across nice geometrical concepts – all this combines to make him highly unsuited to working in the vast hurly-burly of real-life revolution.

These peculiarities of character drive him irresistibly – although he occasionally kicks against it – into the camp of the opportunists and there Martov's talent as a costumier is pressed into service to prepare gorgeous raiment for the muddled effusions of the 'liberdanites'[3] of all kinds.

How many times has Martov, drawn by his genuinely democratic feelings, reached the point of almost concluding an alliance with left social democracy but each time has been repelled by what he calls our uncouthness; each time he has been put off by that sweeping enthusiasm, in which some people find the utmost pleasure and satisfaction, which others regard as diabolical yet fundamentally inherent to the elemental force of revolution, but which is foreign to Martov's temperament.

Once more Martov has fallen into the swamp of 'liberdanism' and his subtle mind is again to be seen flickering above that swamp like a will-o'-the-wisp.

During the first revolution Martov was true to his

nature and fully displayed all the characteristics which I have just tried to describe. I cannot say that during that first clash between the mass of the people and the government he played a leading part as a real political leader: as always he was an excellent analytical journalist, a wrangler, an intra-Party tactician.

136

The next spell of emigration struck Martov a very hard blow; never, perhaps, had his tendency to vacillate been so marked nor probably so agonizing. The right wing of Menshevism soon began to go rotten, deviating into so-called 'liquidationism'. Martov had no wish to be drawn into this petty-bourgeois disintegration of the revolutionary spirit. But the 'liquidators' had a hold on Dan and Dan on Martov and as usual the heavy 'tail' of Menshevism dragged Martov to the bottom. There was a moment when he would literally have made a pact with Lenin, urged to do so by Trotsky and Innokenty,[4] who were dreaming of forming a powerful centre to counter the extreme left and the extreme right.

This line, as we know, was also strongly supported by Plekhanov, but the idyll did not last long, rightism gained the upper hand with Martov and the same discord between Bolsheviks and Mensheviks broke out again.

Martov was then living in Paris. I was told that he had even begun to go slightly to seed, always a lurking danger for *émigrés*. Politics was degenerating into an affair of petty squabbles and a passion for bohemian café life was beginning to threaten him with a diminution of his intellectual powers. However, when the war came Martov not only pulled himself together but from the start took up an extremely resolute position.

There is no doubt that the internationalist wing of the Second International is indebted to Martov for some of its achievements. Martov strongly supported the internationalists by speeches, by articles, by his influence and his connections and drew nearly all the *émigré* Mensheviks (with the exception of the Plekhanovites, who had been regarded until then as leftists but who at the outbreak of war immediately rallied to the imperialist cause of the *Entente*) into supporting the Zimmerwald and Kienthal line, although it is true that at Zimmerwald Martov took up a centrist position and diverged firmly from Lenin and Zinoviev.

Martov was himself again; but it was now that his fatal irresolution emerged once more. Fully aware of the disastrous implications of socialist 'defencism', Martov still hoped to win over the Defencists and could not bring himself to break his organizational links with them. Politically this was the undoing of Martov. It destroyed his moral standing, because Martov might have had a brilliant role to play as the genuine leader and inspirer of a right-wing group within the Communist Party if at that time he had only shown enough resolution to cast his weight on the leftward side of the watershed.

At the beginning of the revolution, after Trotsky's arrival in Russia in May–June, Lenin dreamed of an alliance with Martov, realizing how valuable he could be, but Martov's predominantly right-inclined wavering had already, as far back as his days in Paris, settled his fate in advance – namely to be acknowledged by neither one side nor the other and to be forever out in the cold as an outspoken, honest but powerless one-man opposition!

This tendency rendered Martov politically colourless and as a result he will go down in history as a much dimmer figure than should be the case with a man of his political gifts.

I came much closer to Martov in Switzerland from 1915 to 1916. We were near neighbours, Martov was a frequent guest of my friends the Christys and he and I would often chat not only about politics, over which we invariably quarrelled, but also about literature and cultural matters in general. I admired Martov's taste and the considerable breadth of his interests, although I must admit that, at any rate then, Martov's outlook was a good deal more one-sided than I had expected. He showed no great enthusiasm for art, no great depth of interest in philosophy. He read everything, could talk about everything and talk interestingly, intelligently and at times originally, but somehow he did it all mechanically, his heart was not in it: whenever a newspaper arrived he would break off any conversation and immediately immerse himself in the paper. Even if somebody read aloud something amusing or interesting which aroused Martov's liking or enthusiasm, he would remain screened behind his newspaper as though obsessed by it. Martov only showed real enthusiasm when the talk turned to politics and especially to the narrow field of internal Party politics.

Nevertheless I must admit that in personal relations Martov had considerable charm. There is something intellectually very attractive about him; he has great spontaneity and sincerity which make him a most rewarding companion, and people who are politically neutral always develop a great liking and respect for him. His political allies react, if not with the same fervent adoration that Lenin inspires, then with sincere affection and with their own particular sort of admiration.

I say once more, weighing all that I remember of the man: with deep sadness I am forced to admit that this great man, with his great intellect, has not, due to the inherent limitations of his psychological type, realized one tenth of his potential for constructive influence on politics.

The future? It is idle to attempt to guess. If the communist system wins and consolidates itself, Martov may perhaps have a part to play as a loyal right-wing opposition and may at the same time emerge as one of the creative minds of a new world – which I, for one, sincerely hope will be the case; if, however, there are still to be gaps and lags before the ultimate victory of communism is achieved, Martov will either perish because he is too honest to remain silent in a period of reaction, or he will lose himself hopelessly in the by-ways of revolution, as he is lost at present.*

NOTES

In terms of concrete political achievement Martov was a failure, despite his great services to Russian Social Democracy in its formative years of the 1890s; yet such was the attraction

* And as he was to lose himself right up to his death, of which I learned today during the final correction of my proofs. I am glad to observe that the main lines of my character-sketch correspond exactly with Radek's[5] excellent obituary of Martov in *Izvestiya*.

of his personality that even in the brutally pragmatic world of Russian revolutionary politics, where doctrine and factional allegiances were paramount and a contempt for private feelings was regarded as a cardinal virtue, Lenin never lost his affection for Martov. They had been comrades at the very start of the movement, had been arrested and exiled at the same time, had emigrated and worked in close collaboration on *Iskra*. Their subsequent differences were great. Martov not only led the despised Mensheviks but kept trying to recreate a unified Party which would embrace all shades of opinion, a concept anathema to Lenin; Martov, too, was typical of the bookish, theorizing intelligentsia, a breed Lenin hated although he belonged to it himself; finally Martov could never quite dismiss his scruples (only too well founded) about the ultimate political consequences of giving absolute power to a single, ruthless, rigidly authoritarian Party of the Leninist type. In 1920 Martov went to Berlin with a Menshevik delegation and never came back. As Lenin lay mortally ill in 1923 one of his last articulate remarks (soon afterwards his third stroke deprived him of the power of speech) was to say sadly to his wife: 'They say Martov is dying too.'

1. GRIMM: David Davidovich Grimm (1864–?). Academic lawyer and politician. Leading member of Kadet party. Emigrated after 1917.

2. NOSKE: Gustav Noske. German socialist politician, leading member of the S.P.D. On 23 December 1918, revolutionary troops and armed workers of the extreme left-wing Spartacist League had captured Chancellor Ebert; Hindenburg persuaded loyal troops to free Ebert, which caused street fighting to break out in Berlin between Spartacists and the right-wing *Freikorps*. On 11 January 1919, Gustav Noske led heavily armed detachments into Berlin and retook the capital in the name of the moderate, right-wing socialist government.

3. LIBERDANITES: A term of Bolshevik abuse, compounded of the names of Liber (real name Mark Goldman) and Dan. Liber was one of the leaders of the *Bund* and Dan shared the leadership of the Mensheviks with Martov.

4. INNOKENTY: I. F. Dubrovinsky, alias 'Innokenty'. Early Bolshevik. Member of the Bolshevik Central Committee from 1908. Supported Lenin when the Party threatened

to divide on the issue of reunification with the Mensheviks.

5. RADEK'S EXCELLENT OBITUARY: Karl Bernhardovich Sobelsohn, alias Radek (1885–1939?). Born in Lvov, Austrian Poland, of middle-class Jewish parents. Member of the Polish, German and Russian Social Democratic Parties. Brilliant political journalist. Travelled with Lenin from Switzerland to Russia in the 'sealed train', April 1917. Arrested in Germany, 1918, for revolutionary activity. Returned to Moscow in 1922 as secretary of the Comintern. Joined Trotsky's opposition to Stalin. Expelled from the Party in 1927 and banished to the Urals. Reinstated after writing a panegyric on Stalin. For several years leading Party commentator on foreign affairs in the Soviet Press. Tried during the 'purge' in 1937. Probably died in a concentration camp.

FYODOR IVANOVICH KALININ

It was with profound grief that the workers of Russia marched in procession to the funeral of one of their most remarkable leaders, Fyodor Ivanovich Kalinin. We must welcome the series of decisions taken by the Central Committee of the Proletcult to perpetuate his memory.

Memorials take different forms: they may be statues or editions of a man's works which yet remain majestically dead or at best a closed book.

The scope of F. I. Kalinin's thought was far from being a closed book. He was constantly expanding and developing his ideas, which are like seeds bursting with the power of growth. His true memorial, therefore, is no mere statue but a living cultural process. Comrade Kalinin was both a founder of the proletarian cultural movement and the man whose firm hand launched it on its proper course. Each retreat from that true course will, in my view, undoubtedly be a 'heresy'.

To everything he did the late F. I. Kalinin brought an unusual degree of lucidity. Calmness, an almost classical precision of thought, confidence, a practical approach to every problem were inherent in him and made up, together with his warmth of heart and simplicity, the principal charm of his character.

Comrade Kalinin also brought that same lucidity to the question of proletarian culture, in particular to art, with which, strange as it may seem, he was more concerned than with any other branch of culture.

Fyodor Ivanovich was no artist himself. He was a thinker and organizer. But the problems of art interested him profoundly and came to occupy more and more of his attention. He was as thrilled as a child by every clear manifestation of proletarian art. Indeed, all forms of art were of equal concern to him. And this was no barbarian's fascination with glitter and ornamentation. Kalinin never saw art in the guise of luxury and sensuous pleasure. He was most of all a thinker and organizer when he was concerned with aesthetics. He regarded art as an essential ideological weapon and cherished it as a powerful element in building socialism.

A great deal of confusion reigns in the realm of proletarian aesthetics despite the fact that the attempts to create this aesthetic have been so few and so recent. It is in this field that F. I. Kalinin's ideas have created a canon by which to judge proletarian aesthetics. I repeat that it must grow and develop, but that it should do so on the lines that he has indicated.

Kalinin realized that art is a most subtle process whose roots lie in the very depths of the human psyche. He was not a rationalist, he was not a protagonist of didacticism in works of art, yet at the same time he objected very strongly to the least hint of mystique in the discussion of the social and individual processes of artistic creation. He strove to bring clarity even into the realm of the unconscious, which he regarded as an essential element in creativity.

In his remarkable article 'The Proletariat and Creativity' he writes: 'Many of the believers in mystical intuition are inclined to regard artistic creation as a gift granted only to the elect, who are capable of creating eternal values out of nothing solely by a kind of magical inspiration. This view demonstrates both their high opinion of themselves and their ignorance. All serious research into artistic creativity indicates that it can only occur as a result of intensive work following the acquisition of a rich store of experience. Creation and invention can only be achieved through amassing practical and theoretical knowledge. Every act of discovery or invention is the product of a significant accumulation of qualitative and quantitative experience or material. . . . Art is primarily figurative thinking; it does not prove – it reveals. It therefore cannot be based on logical thinking, if only for the reason that practically every image of any complexity contains a quantity of experience so great that the conscious memory cannot encompass it. Therefore for the artistic process to result in the creation of an image, the repressed memories of the subconscious are an essential adjunct.'

You will observe that comrade Kalinin is anxious to give full credit to the subconscious whilst simultaneously refuting the harmful notion that one can unconsciously create a significant work of art without an effort of the will or exertion of the intellect. And it is just this kind of art which is capable of producing those very works – classic, convincing, as rich in content as they are appropriately clothed in external form – which the masses are bound to demand, indeed are demanding, and which they created in those ages when they really dominated cultural life, such as in the great age of Athens or in renaissance Florence.

Kalinin expected proletarian art to come only from the proletariat. Conscious of the significance of such an art as an instrument of self-awareness of that class which is to save and organize mankind, F. I. Kalinin summoned the proletariat to become proficient in it as soon as possible. 'The intellectuals may think with us,' he goes on to say in the same article, 'and if necessary for us – but feel for us they cannot. . . . The subconscious has its own autonomous existence,' he explains. 'The worker himself is dimly aware of the rustlings within his own soul but only in the moment of concentrated creative application can they assume sharp, clear-cut images at the level of his conscious mind.'

But if in this way a full-blooded art – an art not of the head but from the heart proceeding by way of the head – can be created by the proletariat itself, this by no means implies, in F. I. Kalinin's view, that proletarian culture can be divorced from the cultural achievements of the past. And in that same most interesting article he goes on to say: 'We have two tasks – one basically educational, consisting in the assimilation of the bourgeois inheritance, in defining our proletarian attitude towards it, and in assimilating the elements of proletarian culture already created by the workers' movement. The other task must be the creation of conditions in which the creative powers of the proletariat can emerge in the act of artistic creation itself.'

Kalinin regarded both these tasks as absolutely essential. Speaking of the tasks of the workers' club, to which he attributed great importance in the process of building socialism, he writes: 'There may be those among us who look upon aesthetic needs as something superfluous and unnecessary, especially at such a time of violent struggle. We regard this view as a dangerous illusion. Art is not simply a means of pleasure or embellishment, but is a means of organizing our lives of which we must make use as a weapon in the struggle. And we can only learn to make use of it when we have learned to understand it. Art, as figurative thinking, lies closest of all to the simple thought-processes of ordinary people, who find it hard to understand abstract conceptual thinking. It is art that can most easily enter family life and influence the moulding of human psychology, freeing it from prejudice and thus preparing the workers for the forthcoming struggle for socialist ideals.'

I do not think that anyone could express more clearly and precisely the significance of art for the proletariat in its great struggle.

In the article 'The Way of Proletarian Criticism' F. I. Kalinin attempts to go further and to outline the actual content of proletarian art. 'If the bourgeoisie,' he says, 'brushing aside the thought of the imminent collapse of the capitalist system, has devised for itself a world of pleasant day-dreams and fantasies, through the prism of which it wants to make us see all the events and phenomena of the world, then the proletariat must ruthlessly expose these mirages.' And further: 'In the search for the form and content of proletarian literature, its evaluation – proletarian criticism – must above all approach the matter deliberately and systematically.'

It is comrade Kalinin's view, therefore, that the primary tasks that face proletarian literature are, firstly – the reflection of the contemporary revolutionary mood, secondly – the depiction of the psychology of the progressive worker, which is, in Kalinin's words, complex and not fully susceptible to description by an outsider and is perhaps only expressible in a deeply-felt lyricism. However, it was also obvious to comrade Kalinin (and that is why he welcomed the worker-poet Gastyev)[1] that such lyricism will not be individualistic and that, reflecting its own innermost nature, the progressive proletariat will, to a greater degree than was possible with any other class, express what is common to all mankind, through the heart and mind of the advance-guard of humanity – the working class.

In the article 'Ideological Production' F. Kalinin maintains that the psychology of the proletarian reflects the great era of collective machine production, initiated and considerably developed by capitalism and due henceforth to be developed even further.

In his austere phrasing, which breathes that unique spirit, understood only by a proletarian or by someone who has totally identified himself with the proletariat, comrade Kalinin says: 'Contemporary imperialist capitalism reveals all the signs of impersonality and collectivism. It breeds, in consequence, a collectivist psychology in the industrial proletariat. This emergent structure of industrial society, in which everything is organized by strict calculation based on the demands of the total productive process, in which the worker is only a conscious, disciplined link in the collective chain – it is this form of organization which the proletariat must bring to his ideological and cultural work. By this means we shall contribute to the ultimate formation of a truly proletarian psychology which, though still confused by vestiges of bourgeois mentality, yet bears the marks of a nascent socialist psychology. We must break finally with disorganized spontaneity, replacing it with conscious organization, method and discipline. We too must build our organization on calculation; we must consolidate every crumb of individual experience which, when synthesized, will keep the process moving in the direction of further expansion and development. Thus the proletariat will create the conditions for the ultimate consolidation of socialism.'

This, in the most general terms, is the theory of proletarian art which Kalinin had begun to create. Sharply delimiting the aims of this art both from the current trends of bourgeois artists and from Futurism, he has tried to indicate its course: 'We know,' he wrote in one of his last articles, 'that we must set ourselves one task. It is not easy, but that is no reason for us to evade it. Besides the elimination of the prejudices of bourgeois culture, which have penetrated fairly deeply into the proletariat, we still have to overcome the narrow-minded and inconsistent way of thinking of our worker comrades.' At the same time he expresses a firm confidence that the new-born proletarian art will establish itself and occupy a high position in the general culture of mankind.

Naturally there will inevitably be a stiff fight against both bourgeois prejudices and against the 'heresies' of this embryonic proletarian culture. Although he has physically left the struggle, F. I. Kalinin is morally and intellectually with us and will always be our ally and our support.

NOTES

F. I. Kalinin (not to be confused with M. I. Kalinin; see above, note p. 118) was one of Lunacharsky's working-class protégés. When the occasional workman or autodidact of humble origins worked his way into the upper ranks of the Bolshevik Party, he was made a fuss of as evidence that this was a real workers' Party. One such was Fyodor Ivanovich Kalinin, born the son of a peasant weaver in 1883. Politically active from 1901, when he was arrested and exiled, he led an armed peasant uprising in 1905, for which he was again arrested and sentenced to three years' imprisonment. On release he worked in the illegal underground for the Bolshevik Party for a time, then emigrated. Abroad he was taken up by Bogdanov and Lunacharsky, joined their 'Forward' group and attended their political training school on the isle of Capri – a venture financed by the literary earnings of Maxim Gorky. In 1917 Kalinin returned to Russia. Two years later Lunacharsky gave Kalinin an official post in the Commissariat of Education. Kalinin, who by then had made a certain name as a literary critic, became a leading theoretician of the

'Proletcult' ('Proletarian Culture') movement. He died in 1920, aged only forty-six. Since the suppression of Bogdanov's heterodox ideology under Stalin, Kalinin's writings have faded into complete obscurity.

1. THE WORKER-POET GASTYEV: Alexei Kapitonovich Gastyev (1882–1941). One of the founders, with Bogdanov, of the 'Proletcult' movement. Gastyev belonged to a proletarian school of poets called 'The Smithy'. He hymned the universe as 'a huge factory' and wrote an ode to the machine, 'that Iron Messiah'. For all their self-conscious working-class postures, the 'Smithy' poets owed a heavy literary debt to the Symbolists.

PAVEL BESSALKO

I knew the late Pavel Bessalko from almost the beginning of his literary career. He came to see me with several of his rather feeble juvenilia, none of which, if I am not mistaken, were ever printed. I was a witness to virtually the whole of Bessalko's literary development.

Having survived a terrible spell of imprisonment, sombrely recorded in his grim novel *The Catastrophe*, Bessalko, although at the time a Menshevik, belonged with all his heart to that extremist wing of the workers' movement the core of whose protest was hatred of the intelligentsia and of the Party intelligentsia in particular.

During almost the whole of his stay in Paris as an *émigré*, comrade Pavel was an extreme adherent of the views of Makhaisky.[1] This, however, did not prevent him from becoming my good friend. He and I shared our views, our tastes and our plans.

Gradually his rancour against the intelligentsia abated, but there remained in him a love of his own class, an admirable, quiet pride in being able to say 'I, too, am a proletarian'.

In this sense he was a real man of the working class and he always remained firmly attached to his trade as a fitter although he realized that it hindered him in his literary work.

I believe that of all our worker-writers Bessalko remained most profoundly conscious of being a worker. This emerged in his theoretical articles, for instance, in his vehement and uniquely eloquent attack on the Futurists[2] and in his extremely forceful attempt to oppose the emergent *genre* of peasant poetry with the new proletarian writing.

But what always attracted me to Bessalko and what made me see his figure in a certain sense as symbolic was the fact that, for all the astonishing fidelity of his perception of what it means to be a worker and his passionate devotion to his class, Pavel Bessalko had an extraordinary breadth of outlook. In his view proletarian art should not only describe working-class life (which he did admirably) and the ideals and struggles of the proletariat, but it should express an all-embracing view of the whole world, of all the doings of mankind and of the even vaster world of the imagination, the past, the present and the future: but all from a special vantage point – the vantage point of the proletariat.

And in this Bessalko was extremely successful. Not only in his grim book *The Catastrophe*, not only in his passionately tendentious autobiographical short stories but also in *The Diamonds of the East*, in *Judas*, and in his sketches of Parisian life, some of which recall Murger, some de Maupassant. In all of them Pavel Bessalko remains his working-class self.

Even when writing about his Persian shahs or the gods of Olympus, he still managed, in a manner I found incredible in a man of such restricted knowledge and who was self-taught to a relatively limited degree, to retain the flavour of his chosen location and to write in a style that was in harmony with whatever theme he happened to select.

Universality of outlook combined with an unusually systematic approach to the most varied of subjects – this is what I find most characteristic of Bessalko.

Of course we have only known him as a youth; he had only just grown up, was only just trying his wings, had only just begun to grope with his eager workman's hand for the beautiful shapes surrounding him, trying to illumine them in his own way. We could have expected his talent to have grown to great heights, although no one can say now just what course that rich, tender, profound, avid poetic nature of his might have taken.

We who made the revolution in those terrible years often think with horror and sadness of the immeasurable losses which the proletariat had to suffer as the price of its victory. As a whole class it has actually been numerically reduced. How often one feels a chill when one asks after a dozen or so names – sailors from Kronstadt, heroes of the revolution – and one hears that so-and-so was killed there, so-and-so died there . . .

The countless losses suffered by the working class have affected it in quality as well as quantity. It is enough to reduce one to despair if one did not know that its strength is inexhaustible. Only the elemental inexhaustibility of that multimillion-strong class, only the sight of the serried ranks of the Party intake from the Young Communists coming to take over from us can console us and inspire us with courage.

Pavel Bessalko had set out on a splendid path, mounting only the first steps of the magnificent stairway of what will be a broad and truly proletarian cultural edifice.

But we know that others will follow him, are sure to follow him, are sure to devour greedily the pages he left behind, nourishing themselves on his inspiration; they will carry on the work as though he himself were still working with them, for if there is a truly proletarian concept it is the word 'We'.

The proletarian collective, in a sense that has never existed before, will value the individual no less – indeed more – than any class before it and will give him a wider chance than ever to develop himself and take wing.

That, however, is more a matter for the future. This time of war calls even its winged sons to go whither the future of our whole society is being decided and there to die by bullet or by typhus and it says in consolation: We must win, we shall reward you in full. No single 'I' is too valuable to be spared as a sacrifice for our 'We'.

NOTES

Born in 1880, Pavel Karpovich Bessalko came of peasant stock. Considering that he had virtually no formal education he was endowed with an undoubted natural talent and might have become an author of some stature had he lived longer. Now he is unread and recorded only in works of reference. Like F. I. Kalinin, Bessalko was treasured by Lunacharsky and Bogdanov in their rather artificial 'Proletarian Culture' movement. Arrested in 1907 for revolutionary activity, imprisoned for two years then exiled, Bessalko escaped abroad to reach France in 1911. There he followed his trade as a fitter in a French aircraft factory until 1917, dabbling in writing in his spare time. Violently anti-bourgeois and anti-intelligentsia, Bessalko went back to Russia at the revolution and worked as a journalist. During the Civil War he edited a Red Army newspaper on the Ukrainian front and died of typhus in Kharkov in the autumn of 1920. His published works include two novels, some short stories and a play entitled *The Stonemason.*

1. MAKHAISKY: V. K. Makhaisky, alias A. Volsky (?–1927). A Pole, one-time member of the Polish Socialist Party, Makhaisky adopted a form of Anarcho-Syndicalism. In a number of books published between 1898 and 1905, he argued that knowledge was a means of production and consequently the intelligentsia, with its monopolistic claims to knowledge, was an exploiting class. The working class, according to Makhaisky, should 'expropriate' knowledge from the intelligentsia once the latter had completed the socialist revolution.

2. THE FUTURISTS: An avant-garde literary and artistic movement which in Russia lasted from about 1910 to 1930. Originating in Italy and France, Futurism's aim was the abandonment of the past and the creation of a new art in keeping with the machine age. Its leader and theorist was Viktor Vladimirovich Khlebnikov (1885–1922), although the best known Futurist writer was Vladimir Mayakovsky (1893–1930). They set up a quasi-official organization, the 'Left Front in the Arts' (known by its Russian initials as LEF) but their attitudes were too extreme for most of the Party leadership and LEF was dissolved in 1930, the year of Mayakovsky's suicide. The Futurists' iconoclastic treatment of language and form did have an undoubted effect on subsequent Russian poetry.

BIBLIOGRAPHY

S. V. Utechin, *Concise Encyclopedia of Russia* (London: Dent, 1961).

O. Gankin and H. Fisher, *The Bolsheviks and the World War* (New York: Hoover Library, 1940).

M. T. Florinsky, *Encyclopedia of Russia and the Soviet Union* (New York: McGraw-Hill, 1961).

L. Schapiro, *The Communist Party of the Soviet Union* (London: Eyre & Spottiswoode, 1960).

Harold Shukman, *Lenin and the Russian Revolution* (London: Batsford, 1967).

George Katkov, *Russia 1917: The February Revolution* (London: Longmans, 1967).

Adam B. Ulam, *Lenin and the Bolsheviks* (London: Secker & Warburg, 1966).

Marc Slonim, *Soviet Russian Literature* (New York: O.U.P., 1964).

M. G. Saunders (ed.), *The Soviet Navy* (London: Weidenfeld & Nicolson, 1958).

A. Lunacharsky, *Velikii Perevorot* (Petrograd: Grzhebin, 1919); *Revolutsionnye Silouety* (Moscow: Transposektsiya, 1923); *Revolutsionnye Silouety* (Kiev: Ukrgosizdat, 1924); *Silouety* (Moscow: Molodaya Gvardiya, 1965); *Sobranie Sochinenii v vosmi tomakh* (Moscow: Khudozhestvennaya Literatura, 1963–7).